The

BIBLE'S
PROMISES

FOR
LIFE

E N G L I S H
S T A N D A R D
V E R S I O N

::: CROSSWAY

WHEATON, ILLINOIS

The Bible's Promises for Life

Copyright © 2003 by Good News publishers

Published by Crossway
        1300 Crescent Street
        Wheaton, Illinois

Cover design: Studio Gearbox

First printing 2003

Reprinted with new cover 2011

Printed in the United States of America

Produced with the assistance of The Livingstone Corporation
www.LivingstoneCorp.com

All Scripture taken from the ESV® Bible (*The Holy Bible:
English Standard Version®*). Copyright © 2001 by Crossway.
All rights reserved.

ISBN: 978-1-4335-3171-2

Library of Congress Cataloging-in-Publication Data
The Bible's Promises for Life.
  p. cm.
ISBN 1-58134-499-6
1. Bible—Quotations. I. Crossway Books. II. Title.
BS432.B44212   2003
220.5'208—dc21   2002156206

Crossway is a publishing ministry of Good News Publishers.

| L B | | 20 | 19 | 18 | 17 | 16 | 15 | 14 | 13 | 12 | 11 |
| 14 | 13 | 12 | 11 | 10 | 9 | 8 | 7 | 6 | 5 | 4 | 3 | 2 | 1 |

CONTENTS

FOREWORD

The Bible is the very Word of God. It is God's word of truth and contains the promises of God's eternal love and unchanging character.

We are all looking for promises and truths upon which to build our lives. But human promises and worldly wisdom are still just our promises and wisdom. The Bible's promises and truths are *from God,* the one who made us and who sent his Son to save us from our sins.

The Bible's Promises for Life consists entirely of selections from Scripture, chosen and arranged by topics, to help build a spiritual foundation for your life. Theses passages are all taken from the *Holy Bible: English Standard Version,* a translation of the Bible known for its word-for-word accuracy, clarity, beauty, and readability.

Our sincere prayer for you is that as you read these Scriptures, you will be encouraged and drawn closer to God himself through his son, the Lord Jesus Christ.

The Publishers

ANXIETY

The fear of man lays a snare,
   but whoever trusts in the LORD is safe.

PROVERBS 29:25

Do not be anxious about anything, but in everything by prayer and supplication with thanksgiving let your requests be made known to God. And the peace of God, which surpasses all understanding, will guard your hearts and your minds in Christ Jesus.

PHILIPPIANS 4:6-7

And [Jesus] said to his disciples, "Therefore I tell you, do not be anxious about your life, what you will eat, nor about your body, what you will put on . . . . which of you by being anxious can add a single hour to his span of life? . . . seek his kingdom, and these things will be added to you."

LUKE 12:22, 25, 31

ASSURANCE

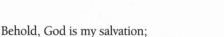

Behold, God is my salvation;
   I will trust, and will not be afraid;
for the LORD GOD is my strength and my song,
   and he has become my salvation.

ISAIAH 12:2

Let us draw near with a true heart in full assurance
of faith, with our hearts sprinkled clean from an evil
conscience and our bodies washed with pure water.

HEBREWS 10:22

But know that the LORD has set apart the godly for
         himself;
   the LORD hears when I call to him.

PSALM 4:3

By this we know that we abide in him and he in us,
because he has given us of his Spirit.

1 JOHN 4:13

For the LORD will be your confidence
   and will keep your foot from being caught.

PROVERBS 3:26

Therefore, since we have been justified by faith, we have peace with God through our Lord Jesus Christ.

ROMANS 5:1

We have this as a sure and steadfast anchor of the soul, a hope that enters into the inner place behind the curtain.

HEBREWS 6:19

I write these things to you who believe in the name of the Son of God that you may know that you have eternal life. And this is the confidence that we have toward him, that if we ask anything according to his will he hears us. And if we know that he hears us in whatever we ask, we know that we have the requests that we have asked of him.

1 JOHN 5:13-15

BAPTISM

Go therefore and make disciples of all nations, baptizing them in the name of the Father and of the Son and of the Holy Spirit.

MATTHEW 28:19

And Peter said to them, "Repent and be baptized every one of you in the name of Jesus Christ for the forgiveness of your sins, and you will receive the gift of the Holy Spirit."

ACTS 2:38

There is one body and one Spirit—just as you were called to the one hope that belongs to your call—one Lord, one faith, one baptism.

EPHESIANS 4:4-5

Blessings from God

Blessed are those whose lawless deeds are forgiven,
and whose sins are covered.

ROMANS 4:7

Praise the Lord! Blessed is the man who fears the
Lord,
who greatly delights in his commandments!

PSALM 112:1

Oh, taste and see that the Lord is good!
Blessed is the man who takes refuge in him!

PSALM 34:8

Blessed is the man who makes
the Lord his trust,
who does not turn to the proud,
to those who go astray after a lie!

PSALM 40:4

Blessed is the one you choose and bring near,
to dwell in your courts!
We shall be satisfied with the goodness of your
house,
the holiness of your temple!

PSALM 65:4

CALLING OF GOD

[God] . . . had set me apart before I was born, and
. . . called me by his grace.

GALATIANS 1:15

[God] saved us and called us to a holy calling, not
because of our works but because of his own purpose and grace, which he gave us in Christ Jesus
before the ages began.

2 TIMOTHY 1:9

And we know that for those who love God all things
work together for good, for those who are called
according to his purpose.

ROMANS 8:28

. . . [and Rebecca was told this] in order that God's
purpose of election might continue, not because of
works but because of his call.

ROMANS 9:11

. . . in order to make known the riches of his glory for
vessels of mercy, which he has prepared beforehand
for glory—even us whom he has called, not from the
Jews only but also from the Gentiles?

ROMANS 9:23-24

CHURCH

You are fellow citizens with the saints and members of the household of God, built on the foundation of the apostles and prophets, Christ Jesus himself being the cornerstone, in whom the whole structure, being joined together, grows into a holy temple in the Lord.

EPHESIANS 2:19-21

[Christ] is the head of the body, the church. He is the beginning, the firstborn from the dead, that in everything he might be preeminent.

COLOSSIANS 1:18

Christ is faithful over God's house as a son. And we are his house if indeed we hold fast our confidence and our boasting in our hope.

HEBREWS 3:6

And when they had appointed elders for them in every church, with prayer and fasting they committed them to the Lord in whom they had believed.

ACTS 14:23

And he gave the apostles, the prophets, the evangelists, the pastors and teachers, to equip the saints for the work of ministry, for building up the body of Christ.

EPHESIANS 4:11-12

Is anyone among you sick? Let him call for the elders of the church, and let them pray over him, anointing him with oil in the name of the Lord. And the prayer of faith will save the one who is sick, and the Lord will raise him up. And if he has committed sins, he will be forgiven.

JAMES 5:14-15

"And I tell you, you are Peter, and on this rock I will build my church, and the gates of hell shall not prevail against it."

MATTHEW 16:18

But you are a chosen race, a royal priesthood, a holy nation, a people for his own possession, that you may proclaim the excellencies of him who called you out of darkness into his marvelous light.

1 PETER 2:9

And let us consider how to stir up one another to love and good works, not neglecting to meet together, as is the habit of some, but encouraging one another, and all the more as you see the Day drawing near.

HEBREWS 10:24-25

And all who believed were together and had all things in common. And they were selling their possessions and belongings and distributing the proceeds to all, as any had need.

ACTS 2:44-45

Comfort

The LORD is a stronghold for the oppressed,
  a stronghold in times of trouble.
And those who know your name put their trust in
    you,
  for you, O LORD, have not forsaken those who
    seek you.

PSALM 9:9-10

Even though I walk through the valley of the shadow
    of death,
  I will fear no evil,
for you are with me;
  your rod and your staff,
    they comfort me.

PSALM 23:4

Fear not, for I am with you;
  be not dismayed, for I am your God;
I will strengthen you, I will help you,
  I will uphold you with my righteous right hand.

ISAIAH 41:10

When the cares of my heart are many,
  your consolations cheer my soul.

PSALM 94:17-19

This is my comfort in my affliction,
   that your promise gives me life.

PSALM 119:50

When I think of your rules from of old,
   I take comfort, O LORD.

PSALM 119:52

Humble yourselves, therefore, under the mighty hand of God so that at the proper time he may exalt you, casting all your anxieties on him, because he cares for you.

1 PETER 5:6-7

Blessed be the God and Father of our Lord Jesus Christ, the Father of mercies and God of all comfort, who comforts us in all our affliction, so that we may be able to comfort those who are in any affliction, with the comfort with which we ourselves are comforted by God.

2 CORINTHIANS 1:3-4

Finally, brothers, rejoice. Aim for restoration, comfort one another, agree with one another, live in peace; and the God of love and peace will be with you.

2 CORINTHIANS 13:11

Now may our Lord Jesus Christ himself, and God our Father, who loved us and gave us eternal comfort and good hope through grace, comfort your hearts and establish them in every good work and word.

2 THESSALONIANS 2:16-17

COMPANIONSHIP

Even though I walk through the valley of the
          shadow of death,
  I will fear no evil,
for you are with me;
  your rod and your staff,
  they comfort me.

                                 PSALM 23:4

And [God] said, "My presence will go with you, and
I will give you rest."

                               EXODUS 33:14

A man of many companions may come to ruin,
  but there is a friend who sticks closer than a
          brother.

                             PROVERBS 18:24

Two are better than one, because they have a good
reward for their toil. For if they fall, one will lift up
his fellow. But woe to him who is alone when he falls
and has not another to lift him up!

                       ECCLESIASTES 4:9-10

A friend loves at all times,
  and a brother is born for adversity.

                           PROVERBS 17:17

COMPASSION

He will tend his flock like a shepherd;
　　he will gather the lambs in his arms;
he will carry them in his bosom,
　　and gently lead those that are with young.

ISAIAH 40:11

A bruised reed he will not break,
　　and a faintly burning wick he will not quench;
　　he will faithfully bring forth justice.

ISAIAH 42:3

When he went ashore he saw a great crowd, and he had compassion on them and healed their sick.

MATTHEW 14:14

For we do not have a high priest who is unable to sympathize with our weaknesses, but one who in every respect has been tempted as we are, yet without sin.

HEBREWS 4:15

Put on then, as God's chosen ones, holy and beloved, compassion, kindness, humility, meekness, and patience.

COLOSSIANS 3:12

CONFESSION OF SIN

Therefore, confess your sins to one another and pray for one another, that you may be healed. The prayer of a righteous person has great power as it is working.

JAMES 5:16

If we say we have no sin, we deceive ourselves, and the truth is not in us. If we confess our sins, he is faithful and just to forgive us our sins and to cleanse us from all unrighteousness. If we say we have not sinned, we make him a liar, and his word is not in us.

1 JOHN 1:8-10

I acknowledged my sin to you,
    and I did not cover my iniquity;
I said, "I will confess my transgressions to the
    LORD,"
    and you forgave the iniquity of my sin.

PSALM 32:5

Have mercy on me, O God,
    according to your steadfast love;
according to your abundant mercy
    blot out my transgressions.
Wash me thoroughly from my iniquity,
    and cleanse me from my sin!

For I know my transgressions,
    and my sin is ever before me.
Against you, you only, have I sinned
    and done what is evil in your sight,
so that you may be justified in your words
    and blameless in your judgment.

PSALM 51:1-4

Therefore, confess your sins to one another and pray
for one another, that you may be healed. The prayer
of a righteous person has great power as it is working.

JAMES 5:16

CONTENTMENT

Behold, what I have seen to be good and fitting is to eat and drink and find enjoyment in all the toil with which one toils under the sun the few days of his life that God has given him, for this is his lot.

ECCLESIASTES 5:18-20

Now there is great gain in godliness with contentment, for we brought nothing into the world, and we cannot take anything out of the world. But if we have food and clothing, with these we will be content.

1 TIMOTHY 6:6-8

Keep your life free from love of money, and be content with what you have, for he has said, "I will never leave you nor forsake you."

HEBREWS 13:5

For the sake of Christ, then, I am content with weaknesses, insults, hardships, persecutions, and calamities. For when I am weak, then I am strong.

2 CORINTHIANS 12:10

Not that I am speaking of being in need, for I have learned in whatever situation I am to be content.

PHILIPPIANS 4:11

If we have food and clothing, with these we will be content.

1 TIMOTHY 6:8

Trust in the LORD, and do good;
    dwell in the land and befriend faithfulness.
Delight yourself in the LORD,
    and he will give you the desires of your heart.

PSALM 37:3-4

"Do not lay up for yourselves treasures on earth . . . but lay up for yourselves treasures in heaven, where neither moth nor rust destroys and where thieves do not break in and steal. For where your treasure is, there your heart will be also."

MATTHEW 6:19-21

COURAGE

Have I not commanded you? Be strong and courageous. Do not be frightened, and do not be dismayed, for the LORD your God is with you wherever you go.

JOSHUA 1:9

For God gave us a spirit not of fear but of power and love and self-control.

2 TIMOTHY 1:7

In the fear of the LORD one has strong confidence,
    and his children will have a refuge.

PROVERBS 14:26

The Lord is my helper;
    I will not fear;
what can man do to me?

HEBREWS 13:6

Wait for the LORD;
    be strong, and let your heart take courage;
    wait for the LORD!

PSALM 27:14

He who dwells in the shelter of the Most High
    will abide in the shadow of the Almighty.

PSALM 91:1

DEATH

Even though I walk through the valley of the
　　　　shadow of death,
　I will fear no evil,
for you are with me;
　　your rod and your staff,
　　they comfort me.

PSALM 23:4

Our God is a God of salvation,
　　and to GOD, the Lord, belong deliverances from
　　　　death.

PSALM 68:20

He will swallow up death forever;
and the Lord GOD will wipe away tears from all faces,
　　and the reproach of his people he will take away
　　　　from all the earth,
for the LORD has spoken.

ISAIAH 25:8

"My sheep hear my voice, and I know them, and
they follow me. I give them eternal life, and they will
never perish, and no one will snatch them out of my
hand."

JOHN 10:27-28

Jesus said to her, "I am the resurrection and the life. Whoever believes in me, though he die, yet shall he live, and everyone who lives and believes in me shall never die."

JOHN 11:25-26

For I am sure that neither death nor life, nor angels nor rulers, nor things present nor things to come, nor powers, nor height nor depth, nor anything else in all creation, will be able to separate us from the love of God in Christ Jesus our Lord.

ROMANS 8:38-39

"Death is swallowed up in victory."
O death, where is your victory?
  O death, where is your sting?
The sting of death is sin, and the power of sin is the law. But thanks be to God, who gives us the victory through our Lord Jesus Christ.

1 CORINTHIANS 15:54-57

Precious in the sight of the LORD
  is the death of his saints.

PSALM 116:15

[God] will wipe away every tear from their eyes, and death shall be no more, neither shall there be mourning nor crying nor pain anymore, for the former things have passed away.

REVELATION 21:4

DELIVERANCE

[Jesus prayed,]
"Lead us not into temptation,
 but deliver us from evil."

MATTHEW 6:13

He delivered us from such a deadly peril, and he will deliver us. On him we have set our hope that he will deliver us again.

2 CORINTHIANS 1:10

[Christ] gave himself for our sins to deliver us from the present evil age, according to the will of our God and Father.

GALATIANS 1:4

[Christ] . . . partook of the same things, that through death he might . . . deliver all those who through fear of death were subject to lifelong slavery.

HEBREWS 2:15

I sought the LORD, and he answered me
 and delivered me from all my fears.

PSALM 34:4

In distress you called, and I delivered you;
 I answered you in the secret place of thunder;
 I tested you at the waters of Meribah.

PSALM 81:7

Then they cried to the LORD in their trouble,
 and he delivered them from their distress.
He brought them out of darkness and the shadow
   of death,
 and burst their bonds apart.

PSALM 107:13-14

No temptation has overtaken you that is not common to man. God is faithful, and he will not let you be tempted beyond your ability, but with the temptation he will also provide the way of escape, that you may be able to endure it.

1 CORINTHIANS 10:13

DESIRE

You will seek the LORD your God and you will find him, if you search after him with all your heart and with all your soul.

DEUTERONOMY 4:29

My soul longs, yes, faints
    for the courts of the LORD;
my heart and flesh sing for joy
    to the living God.

PSALM 84:2

I wait for the LORD, my soul waits,
    and in his word I hope;
my soul waits for the Lord
    more than watchmen for the morning,
    more than watchmen for the morning.

PSALM 130:5-6

In the path of your judgments,
    O LORD, we wait for you;
your name and remembrance
    are the desire of our soul.

ISAIAH 26:8

"Blessed are those who hunger and thirst for righteousness, for they shall be satisfied."

MATTHEW 5:6

DEVOTION

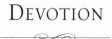

For this very reason, make every effort to supplement your faith with virtue, and virtue with knowledge, and knowledge with self-control, and self-control with steadfastness, and steadfastness with godliness, and godliness with brotherly affection, and brotherly affection with love.

2 PETER 1:5-7

But you, beloved, build yourselves up in your most holy faith; pray in the Holy Spirit; keep yourselves in the love of God, waiting for the mercy of our Lord Jesus Christ that leads to eternal life.

JUDE 20-21

I appeal to you therefore, brothers, by the mercies of God, to present your bodies as a living sacrifice, holy and acceptable to God, which is your spiritual worship. Do not be conformed to this world, but be transformed by the renewal of your mind, that by testing you may discern what is the will of God, what is good and acceptable and perfect.

ROMANS 12:1-2

Whether you eat or drink, or whatever you do, do all to the glory of God.

1 CORINTHIANS 10:31

I have not departed from the commandment of his
      lips;
  I have treasured the words of his mouth more
      than my portion of food.

JOB 23:12

Fear the LORD and serve him faithfully with all your
heart. For consider what great things he has done
for you.

1 SAMUEL 12:24

"No one can serve two masters, for either he will hate
the one and love the other, or he will be devoted to
the one and despise the other. You cannot serve God
and money."

MATTHEW 6:24

For to me to live is Christ, and to die is gain.

PHILIPPIANS 1:21

DISCERNMENT

"The Helper, the Holy Spirit, whom the Father will send in my name . . . will teach you all things and bring to your remembrance all that I have said to you."

JOHN 14:26

"When the Spirit of truth comes, he will guide you into all the truth, for he will not speak on his own authority, but whatever he hears he will speak, and he will declare to you the things that are to come."

JOHN 16:13

And [the Lord] gave the apostles, the prophets, the evangelists, the pastors and teachers, to equip the saints for the work of ministry, for building up the body of Christ, until we all attain to the unity of the faith and of the knowledge of the Son of God . . . so that we may no longer be children, tossed to and fro by the waves and carried about by every wind of doctrine, by human cunning, by craftiness in deceitful schemes.

EPHESIANS 4:11-14

Beloved, do not believe every spirit, but test the spirits to see whether they are from God, for many false prophets have gone out into the world.

1 JOHN 4:1

Teach me good judgment and knowledge,
   for I believe in your commandments.

PSALM 119:66

Trust in the LORD with all your heart,
   and do not lean on your own understanding.
In all your ways acknowledge him,
   and he will make straight your paths.

PROVERBS 3:5-6

The fear of the LORD is the beginning of knowledge;
   fools despise wisdom and instruction.

PROVERBS 1:7

If any of you lacks wisdom, let him ask God, who
gives generously to all without reproach, and it will
be given him.

JAMES 1:5

DISCIPLESHIP

"Whoever does not take his cross and follow me is not worthy of me. Whoever finds his life will lose it, and whoever loses his life for my sake will find it."

MATTHEW 10:38-39

"A disciple is not above his teacher, nor a servant above his master. It is enough for the disciple to be like his teacher, and the servant like his master."

MATTHEW 10:24-25

"Go therefore and make disciples of all nations, baptizing them in the name of the Father and of the Son and of the Holy Spirit, teaching them to observe all that I have commanded you."

MATTHEW 28:19-20

"And whoever gives one of these little ones even a cup of cold water because he is a disciple, truly, I say to you, he will by no means lose his reward."

MATTHEW 10:42

And stretching out his hand toward his disciples, [Jesus] said, "Here are my mother and my brothers!"

MATTHEW 12:49

"If you love me, you will keep my commandments."

JOHN 14:15

DOUBT

Why are you cast down, O my soul,
    and why are you in turmoil within me?
Hope in God; for I shall again praise him,
    my salvation and my God.

PSALM 42:5-6

Has God forgotten to be gracious?
    Has he in anger shut up his compassion?
Then I said, I will appeal to this,
    to the years of the right hand of the Most High.
I will remember the deeds of the LORD;
    yes, I will remember your wonders of old.

PSALM 77:9-11

And [Jesus] said to them, "Why are you afraid, O you
of little faith?" Then he rose and rebuked the winds
and the sea, and there was a great calm.

MATTHEW 8:26

But let him ask in faith, with no doubting, for the
one who doubts is like a wave of the sea that is driven
and tossed by the wind. . . . He is a double-minded
man, unstable in all his ways.

JAMES 1:6, 8

Encouragement

"Well done, good and faithful servant. You have been faithful over a little; I will set you over much. Enter into the joy of your master."

MATTHEW 25:23

Fear not, for I am with you;
    be not dismayed, for I am your God;
I will strengthen you, I will help you,
    I will uphold you with my righteous right hand.

ISAIAH 41:10

Therefore, since we are surrounded by so great a cloud of witnesses, let us also lay aside every weight, and sin which clings so closely, and let us run with endurance the race that is set before us, looking to Jesus, the founder and perfecter of our faith.

HEBREWS 12:1-2a

Let us consider how to stir up one another to love and good works, not neglecting to meet together, as is the habit of some, but encouraging one another, and all the more as you see the Day drawing near.

HEBREWS 10:24-25

ETERNITY

But the LORD is the true God;
 he is the living God and the everlasting King.

JEREMIAH 10:10

Blessed be the LORD, the God of Israel,
 from everlasting to everlasting!

PSALM 41:13

"For God so loved the world, that he gave his only
Son, that whoever believes in him should not perish
but have eternal life."

JOHN 3:16

"Whoever drinks of the water that I will give him will
never be thirsty forever. The water that I will give him
will become in him a spring of water welling up to
eternal life."

JOHN 4:14

Jesus Christ is the same yesterday and today and
forever.

HEBREWS 13:8

When the perishable puts on the imperishable, and
the mortal puts on immortality, then shall come to
pass the saying that is written:

"Death is swallowed up in victory."
"O death, where is your victory?
    O death, where is your sting?"

1 CORINTHIANS 15:54-55

"My sheep hear my voice, and I know them, and they follow me. I give them eternal life, and they will never perish, and no one will snatch them out of my hand."

JOHN 10:27-28

For the wages of sin is death, but the free gift of God is eternal life in Christ Jesus our Lord.

ROMANS 6:23

Then I saw a new heaven and a new earth, for the first heaven and the first earth had passed away, and the sea was no more. . . . And I heard a loud voice from the throne saying, "Behold, the dwelling place of God is with man. He will dwell with them, and they will be his people, and God himself will be with them as their God."

REVELATION 21:1, 3

And night will be no more. They will need no light of lamp or sun, for the Lord God will be their light, and they will reign forever and ever.

REVELATION 22:5

FAITH

And Jesus answered them, "Truly, I say to you, if you have faith and do not doubt, you will . . . say to this mountain, 'Be taken up and thrown into the sea,' [and] it will happen."

MATTHEW 21:21

And to the one who does not work but trusts him who justifies the ungodly, his faith is counted as righteousness.

ROMANS 4:5

By grace you have been saved through faith. And this is not your own doing; it is the gift of God, not a result of works, so that no one may boast.

EPHESIANS 2:8-9

In all circumstances take up the shield of faith, with which you can extinguish all the flaming darts of the evil one.

EPHESIANS 6:16

Now faith is the assurance of things hoped for, the conviction of things not seen.

HEBREWS 11:1

Through the Spirit, by faith, we ourselves eagerly wait for the hope of righteousness.

GALATIANS 5:5

So faith comes from hearing, and hearing through the word of Christ.

ROMANS 10:17

"For God so loved the world, that he gave his only Son, that whoever believes in him should not perish but have eternal life."

JOHN 3:16

Faith by itself, if it does not have works, is dead.

JAMES 2:17

We walk by faith, not by sight.

2 CORINTHIANS 5:7

FAITHFULNESS OF GOD

God is faithful, by whom you were called into the
fellowship of his Son, Jesus Christ our Lord.

1 CORINTHIANS 1:9

O LORD God of hosts,
    who is mighty as you are, O LORD,
    with your faithfulness all around you?

PSALM 89:8

Your steadfast love, O LORD, extends to the heavens,
    your faithfulness to the clouds.

PSALM 36:5

Your faithfulness endures to all generations;
    you have established the earth, and it stands fast.

PSALM 119:90

O LORD, you are my God; I will exalt you; I will
            praise your name,
for you have done wonderful things,
    plans formed of old, faithful and sure.

ISAIAH 25:1

Know therefore that the LORD your God is God, the
faithful God who keeps covenant and steadfast love
with those who love him and keep his command-

ments, to a thousand generations.

DEUTERONOMY 7:9

If we confess our sins, he is faithful and just to forgive us our sins and to cleanse us from all unrighteousness.

1 JOHN 1:9

But the Lord is faithful. He will establish you and guard you against the evil one.

2 THESSALONIANS 3:3

Therefore let those who suffer according to God's will entrust their souls to a faithful Creator while doing good.

1 PETER 4:19

The steadfast love of the LORD never ceases;
    his mercies never come to an end;
they are new every morning;
    great is your faithfulness.

LAMENTATIONS 3:22-23

Let the heavens praise your wonders, O LORD,
    your faithfulness in the assembly of the holy ones!

PSALM 89:5

Let us hold fast the confession of our hope without wavering, for he who promised is faithful.

HEBREWS 10:23

If we are faithless, [God] remains faithful—for he cannot deny himself.

2 TIMOTHY 2:13

FAMILY

Honor your father and your mother, that your days may be long in the land that the LORD your God is giving you.

EXODUS 20:12

A fool despises his father's instruction,
  but whoever heeds reproof is prudent.

PROVERBS 15:5

Grandchildren are the crown of the aged,
  and the glory of children is their fathers.

PROVERBS 17:6

Children, obey your parents in the Lord, for this is right. "Honor your father and mother" (this is the first commandment with a promise), "that it may go well with you and that you may live long in the land." Fathers, do not provoke your children to anger, but bring them up in the discipline and instruction of the Lord.

EPHESIANS 6:1-4

Therefore a man shall leave his father and his mother and hold fast to his wife, and they shall become one flesh. And the man and his wife were both naked and were not ashamed.

GENESIS 2:24-25

He who finds a wife finds a good thing
    and obtains favor from the LORD.

                        PROVERBS 18:22

House and wealth are inherited from fathers,
    but a prudent wife is from the LORD.

                        PROVERBS 19:14

Wives, submit to your husbands, as is fitting in the
Lord. Husbands, love your wives, and do not be
harsh with them.

                        COLOSSIANS 3:18-19

These words that I command you today shall be on
your heart. You shall teach them diligently to your
children, and shall talk of them when you sit in your
house, and when you walk by the way, and when
you lie down, and when you rise.

                        DEUTERONOMY 6:4-9

Whoever spares the rod hates his son,
    but he who loves him is diligent to discipline him.

                        PROVERBS 13:24

Train up a child in the way he should go;
    even when he is old he will not depart from it.

                        PROVERBS 22:6

Husbands, love your wives, as Christ loved the
church and gave himself up for her. . . . He who
loves his wife loves himself.

                        EPHESIANS 5:25,28

FEAR

Even though I walk through the valley of the shadow
        of death,
  I will fear no evil,
for you are with me;
  your rod and your staff,
  they comfort me.

PSALM 23:4

God is our refuge and strength,
  a very present help in trouble.
Therefore we will not fear.

PSALM 46:1-2

Do not be afraid of sudden terror
  or of the ruin of the wicked, when it comes,
for the LORD will be your confidence
  and will keep your foot from being caught.

PROVERBS 3:25-26

The fear of man lays a snare,
  but whoever trusts in the LORD is safe.

PROVERBS 29:25

For I, the LORD your God,
  hold your right hand;

it is I who say to you, "Fear not,
    I am the one who helps you."

ISAIAH 41:13

But now thus says the LORD, he who created you,
        O Jacob,
    he who formed you, O Israel:
Fear not, for I have redeemed you;
    I have called you by name, you are mine.

ISAIAH 43:1

For God gave us a spirit not of fear but of power and love and self-control.

2 TIMOTHY 1:7

He who dwells in the shelter of the Most High
    will abide in the shadow of the Almighty.

PSALM 91:1

The eternal God is your dwelling place,
    and underneath are the everlasting arms.

DEUTERONOMY 33:27

"Peace I leave with you; my peace I give to you. Not as the world gives do I give to you. Let not your hearts be troubled, neither let them be afraid."

JOHN 14:27

FORGIVENESS OF SIN

I acknowledged my sin to you,
and I did not cover my iniquity;
I said, "I will confess my transgressions to the
LORD,"
and you forgave the iniquity of my sin.

PSALM 32:5

For as high as the heavens are above the earth,
so great is his steadfast love toward those who
fear him;
as far as the east is from the west,
so far does he remove our transgressions from
us.

PSALM 103:11-12

If you, O LORD, should mark iniquities,
O Lord, who could stand?
But with you there is forgiveness,
that you may be feared.

PSALM 130:3-4

I, I am he
"who blots out your transgressions for my own
sake,
and I will not remember your sins."

ISAIAH 43:25

He has delivered us from the domain of darkness and transferred us to the kingdom of his beloved Son, in whom we have redemption, the forgiveness of sins.

COLOSSIANS 1:13-14

If we confess our sins, he is faithful and just to forgive us our sins and to cleanse us from all unrighteousness.

1 JOHN 1:9

And you, who were dead in your trespasses and the uncircumcision of your flesh, God made alive together with him, having forgiven us all our trespasses.

COLOSSIANS 2:13

Where there is forgiveness of [sins], there is no longer any offering for sin.

HEBREWS 10:18

Have mercy on me, O God,
    according to your steadfast love;
according to your abundant mercy
    blot out my transgressions.
Wash me thoroughly from my iniquity,
    and cleanse me from my sin!

PSALM 51:1-2

FORGIVING OTHERS

"For if you forgive others their trespasses, your heavenly Father will also forgive you, but if you do not forgive others their trespasses, neither will your Father forgive your trespasses."

MATTHEW 6:14-15

"And whenever you stand praying, forgive, if you have anything against anyone, so that your Father also who is in heaven may forgive you your trespasses."

MARK 11:25

"Judge not, and you will not be judged; condemn not, and you will not be condemned; forgive, and you will be forgiven; give, and it will be given to you."

LUKE 6:37-38

" . . . and forgive us our sins,
    for we ourselves forgive everyone who is
        indebted to us."

LUKE 11:4

Be kind to one another, tenderhearted, forgiving one another, as God in Christ forgave you.

EPHESIANS 4:32

FREEDOM IN CHRIST

"If you abide in my word, you are truly my disciples, and you will know the truth, and the truth will set you free. . . . So if the Son sets you free, you will be free indeed."

JOHN 8:31–32, 36

For freedom Christ has set us free; stand firm therefore, and do not submit again to a yoke of slavery.

GALATIANS 5:1

Do not use your freedom as an opportunity for the flesh, but through love serve one another.

GALATIANS 5:13

Live as people who are free, not using your freedom as a cover-up for evil, but living as servants of God.

1 PETER 2:16

Now the Lord is the Spirit, and where the Spirit of the Lord is, there is freedom.

2 CORINTHIANS 3:17

FRIENDSHIP

Whoever walks with the wise becomes wise,
   but the companion of fools will suffer harm.

PROVERBS 13:20

A friend loves at all times,
   and a brother is born for adversity.

PROVERBS 17:17

Two are better than one, because they have a good reward for their toil. For if they fall, one will lift up his fellow.

ECCLESIASTES 4:9-10

"This is my commandment, that you love one another as I have loved you. Greater love has no one than this, that someone lays down his life for his friends. You are my friends if you do what I command you."

JOHN 15:12-14

Do nothing from rivalry or conceit, but in humility count others more significant than yourselves. Let each of you look not only to his own interests, but also to the interests of others. Have this mind among yourselves, which is yours in Christ Jesus.

PHILIPPIANS 2:3-5

FRUITFULNESS

But the fruit of the Spirit is love, joy, peace, patience, kindness, goodness, faithfulness, gentleness, self-control; against such things there is no law.

GALATIANS 5:22-23

The fruit of the righteous is a tree of life,
    and whoever captures souls is wise.

PROVERBS 11:30

Blessed is the man who walks not in the counsel of
        the wicked,
    nor stands in the way of sinners,
nor sits in the seat of scoffers;
    but his delight is in the law of the LORD,
and on his law he meditates day and night.
    He is like a tree
planted by streams of water
    that yields its fruit in its season,
and its leaf does not wither.
    In all that he does, he prospers.

PSALM 1:1-3

"I am the vine; you are the branches. Whoever abides in me and I in him, he it is that bears much fruit, for apart from me you can do nothing."

JOHN 15:5

GENEROSITY

Each one must give as he has made up his mind, not reluctantly or under compulsion, for God loves a cheerful giver.

2 CORINTHIANS 9:7

Do not neglect to do good and to share what you have, for such sacrifices are pleasing to God.

HEBREWS 13:16

But if anyone has the world's goods and sees his brother in need, yet closes his heart against him, how does God's love abide in him?

1 JOHN 3:17

Blessed is the one who considers the poor!
    In the day of trouble the LORD delivers him.

PSALM 41:1

Whoever has a bountiful eye will be blessed,
    for he shares his bread with the poor.

PROVERBS 22:9

If your enemy is hungry, give him bread to eat,
    and if he is thirsty, give him water to drink,
for you will heap burning coals on his head,
    and the LORD will reward you.

PROVERBS 25:21-22

"For truly, I say to you, whoever gives you a cup of water to drink because you belong to Christ will by no means lose his reward."

MARK 9:41

And [John] answered them, "Whoever has two tunics is to share with him who has none, and whoever has food is to do likewise."

LUKE 3:11

"But give as alms those things that are within, and behold, everything is clean for you."

LUKE 11:41

But if anyone does not provide for his relatives, and especially for members of his household, he has denied the faith and is worse than an unbeliever.

1 TIMOTHY 5:8

Do not neglect to do good and to share what you have, for such sacrifices are pleasing to God.

HEBREWS 13:16

"Truly, I say to you, as you did it to one of the least of these . . . you did it to me."

MATTHEW 25:40

GIFTS OF THE SPIRIT

Now there are varieties of gifts, but the same Spirit; and there are varieties of service, but the same Lord; and there are varieties of activities, but it is the same God who empowers them all in everyone. To each is given the manifestation of the Spirit for the common good.

1 CORINTHIANS 12:4-6

"If you then, who are evil, know how to give good gifts to your children, how much more will the heavenly Father give the Holy Spirit to those who ask him!"

LUKE 11:13

As each has received a gift, use it to serve one another, as good stewards of God's varied grace.

1 PETER 4:10

Having gifts that differ according to the grace given to us, let us use them: if prophecy, in proportion to our faith; if service, in our serving; the one who teaches, in his teaching; the one who exhorts, in his exhortation; the one who contributes, in generosity; the one who leads, with zeal; the one who does acts of mercy, with cheerfulness.

ROMANS 12:6-8

GLORY OF GOD

The heavens declare the glory of God,
    and the sky above proclaims his handiwork.

PSALM 19:1

And the Word became flesh and dwelt among us,
and we have seen his glory, glory as of the only Son
from the Father, full of grace and truth.

JOHN 1:14

Who is like you, O LORD, among the gods?
    Who is like you, majestic in holiness,
    awesome in glorious deeds, doing wonders?

EXODUS 15:11

May the glory of the LORD endure forever;
    may the LORD rejoice in his works.

PSALM 104:31

For all have sinned and fall short of the glory of God.

ROMANS 3:23

So, whether you eat or drink, or whatever you do, do
all to the glory of God.

1 CORINTHIANS 10:31

GODLINESS

While bodily training is of some value, godliness is of value in every way, as it holds promise for the present life and also for the life to come.

1 TIMOTHY 4:8

Make every effort to supplement your faith with virtue, and virtue with knowledge, and knowledge with self-control, and self-control with steadfastness, and steadfastness with godliness.

2 PETER 1:5-6

Now there is great gain in godliness with contentment.

1 TIMOTHY 6:6

As for you, O man of God . . . Pursue righteousness, godliness, faith, love, steadfastness, gentleness.

1 TIMOTHY 6:11

Have nothing to do with irreverent, silly myths. Rather train yourself for godliness.

1 TIMOTHY 4:7

Indeed, all who desire to live a godly life in Christ Jesus will be persecuted.

2 TIMOTHY 3:12

GOODNESS OF GOD

Oh, taste and see that the LORD is good!
  Blessed is the man who takes refuge in him!

PSALM 34:8

And we know that for those who love God all things
work together for good, for those who are called
according to his purpose.

ROMANS 8:28

Every good gift and every perfect gift is from above,
coming down from the Father of lights with whom
there is no variation or shadow due to change.

JAMES 1:17

Good and upright is the LORD;
  therefore he instructs sinners in the way.

PSALM 25:8

The LORD is good,
  a stronghold in the day of trouble;
he knows those who take refuge in him.

NAHUM 1:7

The LORD is good to all,
  and his mercy is over all that he has made.

PSALM 145:9

GRACE OF GOD

The LORD passed before him and proclaimed, "The LORD, the LORD, a God merciful and gracious, slow to anger, and abounding in steadfast love and faithfulness, keeping steadfast love for thousands, forgiving iniquity and transgression and sin, but who will by no means clear the guilty, visiting the iniquity of the fathers on the children and the children's children, to the third and the fourth generation.

EXODUS 34:6-7

All have sinned and fall short of the glory of God, and are justified by his grace as a gift, through the redemption that is in Christ Jesus.

ROMANS 3:23-24

And [the Lord] said, "I will make all my goodness pass before you and will proclaim before you my name 'The LORD.' And I will be gracious to whom I will be gracious, and will show mercy on whom I will show mercy."

EXODUS 33:19

The LORD is gracious and merciful,
    slow to anger and abounding in steadfast love.
The LORD is good to all,
    and his mercy is over all that he has made.

PSALM 145:8-9

The grace of God has appeared, bringing salvation for all people.

TITUS 2:11

I give thanks to my God always for you because of the grace of God that was given you in Christ Jesus.

1 CORINTHIANS 1:4

By grace you have been saved through faith. And this is not your own doing; it is the gift of God.

EPHESIANS 2:8

Therefore the LORD waits to be gracious to you,
and therefore he exalts himself to show mercy
to you.
For the LORD is a God of justice;
blessed are all those who wait for him.

ISAIAH 30:18

Grace was given to each one of us according to the measure of Christ's gift.

EPHESIANS 4:7

Put false ways far from me
and graciously teach me your law!

PSALM 119:29

God shows his love for us in that while we were still sinners, Christ died for us.

ROMANS 5:8

Gratefulness

Offer to God a sacrifice of thanksgiving.

PSALM 50:14

Whatever you do, in word or deed, do everything in the name of the Lord Jesus, giving thanks to God the Father through him.

COLOSSIANS 3:17

Give thanks in all circumstances; for this is the will of God in Christ Jesus for you.

1 THESSALONIANS 5:18

Sing praises to the LORD, O you his saints,
    and give thanks to his holy name.

PSALM 30:4

Praise the LORD! Oh give thanks to the LORD, for he
        is good,
    for his steadfast love endures forever!

PSALM 106:1

Enter his gates with thanksgiving,
    and his courts with praise!
    Give thanks to him; bless his name!

PSALM 100:4

GREED

But those who desire to be rich fall into temptation, into a snare, into many senseless and harmful desires that plunge people into ruin and destruction. For the love of money is a root of all kinds of evils. It is through this craving that some have wandered away from the faith and pierced themselves with many pangs.

1 TIMOTHY 6:9-10

Put to death therefore what is earthly in you: sexual immorality, impurity, passion, evil desire, and covetousness, which is idolatry.

COLOSSIANS 3:5

And he said to them, "Take care, and be on your guard against all covetousness, for one's life does not consist in the abundance of his possessions."

LUKE 12:15

You shall not covet your neighbor's house; you shall not covet your neighbor's wife, or his male servant, or his female servant, or his ox, or his donkey, or anything that is your neighbor's.

EXODUS 20:17

For you may be sure of this, that everyone who is sexually immoral or impure, or who is covetous (that is, an idolater), has no inheritance in the kingdom of Christ and God.

EPHESIANS 5:5

Do not love the world or the things in the world. If anyone loves the world, the love of the Father is not in him. For all that is in the world—the desires of the flesh and the desires of the eyes and pride in possessions—is not from the Father but is from the world. And the world is passing away along with its desires, but whoever does the will of God abides forever.

1 JOHN 2:15-17

"No one can serve two masters, for either he will hate the one and love the other, or he will be devoted to the one and despise the other. You cannot serve God and money."

MATTHEW 6:24

HAPPINESS

~~~

You make known to me the path of life;
    in your presence there is fullness of joy;
    at your right hand are pleasures forevermore.

<div align="right">

PSALM 16:11

</div>

Then our mouth was filled with laughter,
    and our tongue with shouts of joy;
then they said among the nations,
"The LORD has done great things for them."
The LORD has done great things for us;
    we are glad.

<div align="right">

PSALM 126:2-3

</div>

I will greatly rejoice in the LORD;
    my soul shall exult in my God,
for he has clothed me with the garments of
        salvation;
    he has covered me with the robe of
        righteousness.

<div align="right">

ISAIAH 61:10

</div>

And the angel said to them, "Fear not, for behold, I
bring you good news of a great joy that will be for all
the people. For unto you is born this day in the city
of David a Savior, who is Christ the Lord."

<div align="right">

LUKE 2:10-11

</div>

Though you have not seen him, you love him. Though you do not now see him, you believe in him and rejoice with joy that is inexpressible and filled with glory, obtaining the outcome of your faith, the salvation of your souls.

1 PETER 1:8-9

Behold, how good and pleasant it is
    when brothers dwell in unity!

PSALM 133:1

Rejoice in the Lord always; again I will say, Rejoice.

PHILIPPIANS 4:4

"Blessed are you when others revile you and persecute you and utter all kinds of evil against you falsely on my account. Rejoice and be glad, for your reward is great in heaven, for so they persecuted the prophets who were before you."

MATTHEW 5:11-12

HEALTH

While bodily training is of some value, godliness is of value in every way, as it holds promise for the present life and also for the life to come.

1 TIMOTHY 4:8

Beloved, I pray that all may go well with you and that you may be in good health, as it goes well with your soul.

3 JOHN 2

We know that if the tent, which is our earthly home, is destroyed, we have a building from God, a house not made with hands, eternal in the heavens.

2 CORINTHIANS 5:1

A joyful heart is good medicine,
    but a crushed spirit dries up the bones.

PROVERBS 17:22

Is anyone among you sick? Let him call for the elders of the church, and let them pray over him, anointing him with oil in the name of the Lord. And the prayer of faith will save the one who is sick, and the Lord will raise him up.

JAMES 5:14-15

HEAVEN

"In my Father's house are many rooms. If it were not so, would I have told you that I go to prepare a place for you? And if I go and prepare a place for you, I will come again and will take you to myself, that where I am you may be also."

JOHN 14:2-3

"Then the King will say to those on his right, 'Come, you who are blessed by my Father, inherit the kingdom prepared for you from the foundation of the world.'"

MATTHEW 25:34

For here [on earth] we have no lasting city, but we seek the city that is to come.

HEBREWS 13:14

[God] will wipe away every tear from their eyes, and death shall be no more, neither shall there be mourning nor crying nor pain anymore, for the former things have passed away.

REVELATION 21:4

"Lay up for yourselves treasures in heaven, where neither moth nor rust destroys and where thieves do not break in and steal."

MATTHEW 6:20

HONESTY

Lying lips are an abomination to the LORD,
    but those who act faithfully are his delight.

PROVERBS 12:22

Take pains to have a clear conscience toward both God and man.

ACTS 24:16

Now therefore fear the LORD and serve him in sincerity and in faithfulness.

JOSHUA 24:14

Show yourself in all respects to be a model of good works, and in your teaching show integrity, dignity.

TITUS 2:7

Let the thief no longer steal, but rather let him labor, doing honest work with his own hands, so that he may have something to share with anyone in need.

EPHESIANS 4:28

The aim of our charge is love that issues from a pure heart and a good conscience and a sincere faith.

1 TIMOTHY 1:5

You shall not bear false witness against your neighbor.

EXODUS 20:16

Justice, and only justice, you shall follow, that you may live and inherit the land that the LORD your God is giving you.

DEUTERONOMY 16:20

A false balance is an abomination to the LORD,
    but a just weight is his delight.

PROVERBS 11:1

"You know the commandments: 'Do not murder, Do not commit adultery, Do not steal, Do not bear false witness, Do not defraud, Honor your father and mother.'"

MARK 10:19

Therefore, having put away falsehood, let each one of you speak the truth with his neighbor, for we are members one of another.

EPHESIANS 4:25

He who has clean hands and a pure heart,
    who does not lift up his soul to what is false
    and does not swear deceitfully.
He will receive blessing from the LORD
    and righteousness from the God of his salvation.

PSALM 24:4-5

HONOR

"If anyone serves me, he must follow me; and where I am, there will my servant be also. If anyone serves me, the Father will honor him."

JOHN 12:26

Honor everyone. Love the brotherhood. Fear God.

1 PETER 2:17

Honor your father and your mother, that your days may be long in the land that the LORD your God is giving you.

EXODUS 20:12

The fear of the LORD is instruction in wisdom,
and humility comes before honor.

PROVERBS 15:33

The reward for humility and fear of the LORD
is riches and honor and life.

PROVERBS 22:4

Repay no one evil for evil, but give thought to do what is honorable in the sight of all.

ROMANS 12:17

One's pride will bring him low,
but he who is lowly in spirit will obtain honor.

PROVERBS 29:23

HOPE

Hope that is seen is not hope. For who hopes for what he sees? But if we hope for what we do not see, we wait for it with patience.

ROMANS 8:24-25

Why are you cast down, O my soul,
    and why are you in turmoil within me?
Hope in God; for I shall again praise him,
    my salvation and my God.

PSALM 42:11

For you, O Lord, are my hope,
    my trust, O LORD, from my youth.

PSALM 71:5

For whatever was written in former days was written for our instruction, that through endurance and through the encouragement of the Scriptures we might have hope.

ROMANS 15:4

May the God of hope fill you with all joy and peace in believing, so that by the power of the Holy Spirit you may abound in hope.

ROMANS 15:13

Let us hold fast the confession of our hope without wavering, for he who promised is faithful.

HEBREWS 10:23

Blessed be the God and Father of our Lord Jesus Christ! According to his great mercy, he has caused us to be born again to a living hope through the resurrection of Jesus Christ from the dead.

1 PETER 1:3

Therefore, preparing your minds for action, and being sober-minded, set your hope fully on the grace that will be brought to you at the revelation of Jesus Christ.

1 PETER 1:13

Rejoice in hope, be patient in tribulation, be constant in prayer.

ROMANS 12:12

So now faith, hope, and love abide, these three; but the greatest of these is love.

1 CORINTHIANS 13:13

But in your hearts regard Christ the Lord as holy, always being prepared to make a defense to anyone who asks you for a reason for the hope that is in you.

1 PETER 3:15

Faith is the assurance of things hoped for, the conviction of things not seen.

HEBREWS 11:1

IDENTITY

So God created man in his own image,
   in the image of God he created him;
   male and female he created them.

GENESIS 1:27

Do you not know that you are God's temple and that
God's Spirit dwells in you?

1 CORINTHIANS 3:16

If anyone is in Christ, he is a new creation. The old
has passed away; behold, the new has come.

2 CORINTHIANS 5:17

Because you are sons, God has sent the Spirit of his
Son into our hearts, crying, "Abba! Father!" So you
are no longer a slave, but a son, and if a son, then an
heir through God.

GALATIANS 4:6-7

So then you are no longer strangers and aliens, but
you are fellow citizens with the saints and members
of the household of God.

EPHESIANS 2:19

IDOLATRY

You shall have no other gods before me.

EXODUS 20:3

Little children, keep yourselves from idols.

1 JOHN 5:21

Put to death therefore what is earthly in you: sexual immorality, impurity, passion, evil desire, and covetousness, which is idolatry.

COLOSSIANS 3:5

But as for the cowardly, the faithless, the detestable, as for murderers, the sexually immoral, sorcerers, idolaters, and all liars, their portion will be in the lake that burns with fire and sulfur, which is the second death.

REVELATION 21:8

Therefore, my beloved, flee from idolatry.

1 CORINTHIANS 10:14

Do you not know that if you present yourselves to anyone as obedient slaves, you are slaves of the one whom you obey, either of sin, which leads to death, or of obedience, which leads to righteousness?

ROMANS 6:16

INSPIRATION OF GOD'S WORD

All Scripture is breathed out by God and profitable for teaching, for reproof, for correction, and for training in righteousness.

2 TIMOTHY 3:16

No prophecy was ever produced by the will of man, but men spoke from God as they were carried along by the Holy Spirit.

2 PETER 1:21

Your word is a lamp to my feet
and a light to my path.

PSALM 119:105

The law of the LORD is perfect,
reviving the soul;
the testimony of the LORD is sure,
making wise the simple;
the precepts of the LORD are right,
rejoicing the heart;
the commandment of the LORD is pure,
enlightening the eyes.

PSALM 19:7-8

INTEGRITY

We aim at what is honorable not only in the Lord's sight but also in the sight of man.

2 CORINTHIANS 8:21

The integrity of the upright guides them,
> but the crookedness of the treacherous destroys
> them.

PROVERBS 11:3

You shall not steal; you shall not deal falsely; you shall not lie to one another.

LEVITICUS 19:11

Truthful lips endure forever,
> but a lying tongue is but for a moment.

PROVERBS 12:19

"One who is faithful in a very little is also faithful in much, and one who is dishonest in a very little is also dishonest in much."

LUKE 16:10

Whatever you do, work heartily, as for the Lord and not for men.

COLOSSIANS 3:23

You shall do no wrong in judgment, in measures of length or weight or quantity.

LEVITICUS 19:35

"Let what you say be simply 'Yes' or 'No'; anything more than this comes from evil."

MATTHEW 5:37

Whoever speaks the truth gives honest evidence,
but a false witness utters deceit.

PROVERBS 12:17

Better is a poor person who walks in his integrity
than one who is crooked in speech and is a fool.

PROVERBS 19:1

Finally, brothers, whatever is true, whatever is honorable, whatever is just, whatever is pure, whatever is lovely, whatever is commendable, if there is any excellence, if there is anything worthy of praise, think about these things.

PHILIPPIANS 4:8

INTERCESSION

If someone sins against a man, God will mediate for him, but if someone sins against the LORD, who can intercede for him?

1 SAMUEL 2:25

I urge that supplications, prayers, intercessions, and thanksgivings be made for all people, for kings and all who are in high positions, that we may lead a peaceful and quiet life, godly and dignified in every way.

1 TIMOTHY 2:1-2

Pray for us, for we are sure that we have a clear conscience, desiring to act honorably in all things.

HEBREWS 13:18

Is anyone among you sick? Let him call for the elders of the church, and let them pray over him, anointing him with oil in the name of the Lord.

JAMES 5:14

If anyone sees his brother committing a sin not leading to death, he shall ask, and God will give him life.

1 JOHN 5:16

Consequently, [Jesus] is able to save to the uttermost those who draw near to God through him, since he always lives to make intercession for them.

HEBREWS 7:25

Likewise the Spirit helps us in our weakness. For we do not know what to pray for as we ought, but the Spirit himself intercedes for us with groanings too deep for words.

ROMANS 8:26

Who is to condemn? Christ Jesus is the one who died—more than that, who was raised—who is at the right hand of God, who indeed is interceding for us.

ROMANS 8:34

JOY

And the angel said to them, "Fear not, for behold, I bring you good news of a great joy that will be for all the people."

LUKE 2:10

To the one who pleases him God has given wisdom and knowledge and joy.

ECCLESIASTES 2:26

The fruit of the Spirit is love, joy, peace, patience, kindness, goodness, faithfulness.

GALATIANS 5:22

Light is sown for the righteous,
    and joy for the upright in heart.

PSALM 97:11

You make known to me the path of life;
    in your presence there is fullness of joy;
    at your right hand are pleasures forevermore.

PSALM 16:11

Rejoice in hope, be patient in tribulation, be constant in prayer.

ROMANS 12:12

Deceit is in the heart of those who devise evil,
    but those who plan peace have joy.

PROVERBS 12:20

"Well done, good and faithful servant. You have
been faithful over a little; I will set you over much.
Enter into the joy of your master."

MATTHEW 25:21

Therefore, since we are surrounded by so great a
cloud of witnesses, let us also lay aside every weight,
and sin which clings so closely, and let us run with
endurance the race that is set before us, looking to
Jesus, the founder and perfecter of our faith, who for
the joy that was set before him endured the cross,
despising the shame, and is seated at the right hand
of the throne of God.

HEBREWS 12:1-2

Rejoice in the Lord always; again I will say, Rejoice.

PHILIPPIANS 4:4

Count it all joy, my brothers, when you meet trials
of various kinds.

JAMES 1:2

The kingdom of God is not a matter of eating and
drinking but of righteousness and peace and joy in
the Holy Spirit.

ROMANS 14:17

JUDGING

"Judge not, that you be not judged. For with the judgment you pronounce you will be judged, and with the measure you use it will be measured to you."

MATTHEW 7:1-2

The LORD sees not as man sees: man looks on the outward appearance, but the LORD looks on the heart.

1 SAMUEL 16:7

"Judge not, and you will not be judged; condemn not, and you will not be condemned; forgive, and you will be forgiven."

LUKE 6:37

Why do you pass judgment on your brother? Or you, why do you despise your brother? For we will all stand before the judgment seat of God.

ROMANS 14:10

Therefore you have no excuse, O man, every one of you who judges. For in passing judgment on another you condemn yourself, because you, the judge, practice the very same things.

ROMANS 2:1

JUSTICE

He has told you, O man, what is good;
and what does the LORD require of you
but to do justice, and to love kindness,
and to walk humbly with your God?

MICAH 6:8

Learn to do good; seek justice,
correct oppression;
bring justice to the fatherless,
plead the widow's cause.

ISAIAH 1:17

But let justice roll down like waters,
and righteousness like an ever-flowing stream.

AMOS 5:24

When justice is done, it is a joy to the righteous
but terror to evildoers.

PROVERBS 21:15

Finally, brothers, whatever is true, whatever is honorable, whatever is just, whatever is pure, whatever
is lovely, whatever is commendable, if there is any
excellence, if there is anything worthy of praise,
think about these things.

PHILIPPIANS 4:8

JUSTIFICATION

We know that a person is not justified by works of the law but through faith in Jesus Christ, so we also have believed in Christ Jesus, in order to be justified by faith in Christ and not by works of the law, because by works of the law no one will be justified.

GALATIANS 2:16

Now it is evident that no one is justified before God by the law, for "The righteous shall live by faith."

GALATIANS 3:11

I do not nullify the grace of God, for if justification were through the law, then Christ died for no purpose.

GALATIANS 2:21

Truly, truly, I say to you, whoever hears my word and believes him who sent me has eternal life. He does not come into judgment, but has passed from death to life.

JOHN 5:24

Therefore, since we have been justified by faith, we have peace with God through our Lord Jesus Christ.

ROMANS 5:1

LOVE OF GOD

God shows his love for us in that while we were still sinners, Christ died for us.

ROMANS 5:8

"For God so loved the world, that he gave his only Son, that whoever believes in him should not perish but have eternal life."

JOHN 3:16

Therefore be imitators of God, as beloved children. And walk in love, as Christ loved us and gave himself up for us, a fragrant offering and sacrifice to God.

EPHESIANS 5:1-2

I will sing of the steadfast love of the LORD, forever; with my mouth I will make known your faithfulness to all generations.

PSALM 89:1

Beloved, let us love one another, for love is from God, and whoever loves has been born of God and knows God. Anyone who does not love does not know God, because God is love.

1 JOHN 4:7-8

This is love, not that we have loved God but that he loved us and sent his Son to be the propitiation for our sins. . . . If we love one another, God abides in us and his love is perfected in us.

1 JOHN 4:10, 12

The LORD passed before him and proclaimed, "The LORD, the LORD, a God merciful and gracious, slow to anger, and abounding in steadfast love and faithfulness, keeping steadfast love for thousands, forgiving iniquity and transgression and sin, but who will by no means clear the guilty, visiting the iniquity of the fathers on the children and the children's children, to the third and the fourth generation."

EXODUS 34:6-7

We have come to know and to believe the love that God has for us. God is love, and whoever abides in love abides in God, and God abides in him.

1 JOHN 4:16

The steadfast love of the LORD never ceases;
     his mercies never come to an end;
they are new every morning;
     great is your faithfulness.

LAMENTATIONS 3:22-23

For the Lord disciplines the one he loves,
     and chastises every son whom he receives.

HEBREWS 12:6

We love because he first loved us.

1 JOHN 4:19

MEDIATION

~~~~~~

There is one God, and there is one mediator between God and men, the man Christ Jesus.

1 TIMOTHY 2:5

Jesus said to him, "I am the way, and the truth, and the life. No one comes to the Father except through me."

JOHN 14:6

[Jesus said,] "And I will ask the Father, and he will give you another Helper, to be with you forever."

JOHN 14:16

Therefore, since we have been justified by faith, we have peace with God through our Lord Jesus Christ.

ROMANS 5:1

Who is to condemn? Christ Jesus is the one who died—more than that, who was raised—who is at the right hand of God, who indeed is interceding for us.

ROMANS 8:34

But if anyone does sin, we have an advocate with the Father, Jesus Christ the righteous. He is the propitiation for our sins, and not for ours only but also for the sins of the whole world.

1 JOHN 2:1-2

MEEKNESS

"Blessed are the meek, for they shall inherit the earth."

MATTHEW 5:5

"Take my yoke upon you, and learn from me, for I am gentle and lowly in heart, and you will find rest for your souls."

MATTHEW 11:29

But as for you, O man of God, flee these things. Pursue righteousness, godliness, faith, love, steadfastness, gentleness.

1 TIMOTHY 6:11

Who is wise and understanding among you? By his good conduct let him show his works in the meekness of wisdom.

JAMES 3:13

Put on then, as God's chosen ones, holy and beloved, compassion, kindness, humility, meekness, and patience.

COLOSSIANS 3:12

MERCY

❧

But you, O Lord, are a God merciful and gracious,
   slow to anger and abounding in steadfast love
      and faithfulness.

PSALM 86:15

"Be merciful, even as your Father is merciful."

LUKE 6:36

Put on then, as God's chosen ones, holy and
beloved, compassion, kindness, humility, meekness,
and patience.

COLOSSIANS 3:12

For the LORD your God is a merciful God. He will not
leave you or destroy you or forget the covenant with
your fathers that he swore to them.

DEUTERONOMY 4:31

"Blessed are the merciful, for they shall receive
      mercy."

MATTHEW 5:7

With the merciful you show yourself merciful;
   with the blameless man you show yourself
      blameless.

2 SAMUEL 22:26

For [God] says to Moses, "I will have mercy on whom I have mercy, and I will have compassion on whom I have compassion."

ROMANS 9:15

For judgment is without mercy to one who has shown no mercy. Mercy triumphs over judgment.

JAMES 2:13

He has told you, O man, what is good;
and what does the LORD require of you
but to do justice, and to love kindness,
and to walk humbly with your God?

MICAH 6:8

If my people who are called by my name humble themselves, and pray and seek my face and turn from their wicked ways, then I will hear from heaven and will forgive their sin and heal their land.

2 CHRONICLES 7:14

Remember your mercy, O LORD, and your steadfast love,
for they have been from of old.

PSALM 25:6

The LORD is gracious and merciful,
slow to anger and abounding in steadfast love.
The LORD is good to all,
and his mercy is over all that he has made.

PSALM 145:8-9

OBEDIENCE

[Jesus said,] "If you keep my commandments, you will abide in my love, just as I have kept my Father's commandments and abide in his love."

JOHN 15:10

If we say we have fellowship with [God] while we walk in darkness, we lie and do not practice the truth.

1 JOHN 1:6

Children, obey your parents in the Lord, for this is right. "Honor your father and mother" (this is the first commandment with a promise), "that it may go well with you and that you may live long in the land."

EPHESIANS 6:1-4

[Jesus said,] "My sheep hear my voice, and I know them, and they follow me."

JOHN 10:27

Let every person be subject to the governing authorities. For there is no authority except from God, and those that exist have been instituted by God.

ROMANS 13:1

[Jesus said,] "If you love me, you will keep my commandments."

JOHN 14:15

[Jesus said,] "For whoever does the will of my Father in heaven is my brother and sister and mother."

MATTHEW 12:50

Jesus answered him, "If anyone loves me, he will keep my word, and my Father will love him, and we will come to him and make our home with him."

JOHN 14:23

As obedient children, do not be conformed to the passions of your former ignorance.

1 PETER 1:14

Whatever we ask we receive from [Christ], because we keep his commandments and do what pleases him. . . . Whoever keeps his commandments abides in him, and he in them. And by this we know that he abides in us, by the Spirit whom he has given us.

1 JOHN 3:22, 24

PAIN

~~~

To the woman he said,
"I will surely multiply your pain in childbearing;
    in pain you shall bring forth children.
Your desire shall be for your husband,
    and he shall rule over you."
   And to Adam he said,
"Because you have listened to the voice of your wife
    and have eaten of the tree
of which I commanded you,
    'You shall not eat of it,'
cursed is the ground because of you;
    in pain you shall eat of it all the days of your life."

GENESIS 3:16-17

For the moment all discipline seems painful rather than pleasant, but later it yields the peaceful fruit of righteousness to those who have been trained by it.

HEBREWS 12:11

[God] will wipe away every tear from their eyes, and death shall be no more, neither shall there be mourning nor crying nor pain anymore, for the former things have passed away.

REVELATION 21:4

PATIENCE

But if we hope for what we do not see, we wait for it with patience.

ROMANS 8:25

Love is patient and kind; love does not envy or boast.

1 CORINTHIANS 13:4

Rejoice in hope, be patient in tribulation, be constant in prayer.

ROMANS 12:12

And let us not grow weary of doing good, for in due season we will reap, if we do not give up.

GALATIANS 6:9

I waited patiently for the LORD;
  he inclined to me and heard my cry.

PSALM 40:1

Be patient, therefore, brothers, until the coming of the Lord. See how the farmer waits for the precious fruit of the earth, being patient about it, until it receives the early and the late rains.

JAMES 5:7

PEACE

"Glory to God in the highest,
   and on earth peace among those with whom he
      is pleased!"

LUKE 2:14

May the LORD give strength to his people!
   May the LORD bless his people with peace!

PSALM 29:11

Therefore, since we have been justified by faith, we
have peace with God through our Lord Jesus Christ.

ROMANS 5:1

"Agree with God, and be at peace;
   thereby good will come to you."

JOB 22:21

[Jesus said,] "I have said these things to you, that in me
you may have peace. In the world you will have tribulation. But take heart; I have overcome the world."

JOHN 16:33

But the fruit of the Spirit is love, joy, peace, patience,
kindness, goodness, faithfulness, gentleness, self-
control; against such things there is no law.

GALATIANS 5:22-23

Great peace have those who love your law;
    nothing can make them stumble.

PSALM 119:165

And the effect of righteousness will be peace,
    and the result of righteousness, quietness and
        trust forever.

ISAIAH 32:17

For the kingdom of God is not a matter of eating and
drinking but of righteousness and peace and joy in
the Holy Spirit.

ROMANS 14:17

"There is no peace," says the LORD, "for the wicked."

ISAIAH 48:22

Let the peace of Christ rule in your hearts, to which
indeed you were called in one body. And be thankful.

COLOSSIANS 3:15

[Jesus said,] "Peace I leave with you; my peace I
give to you. Not as the world gives do I give to you.
Let not your hearts be troubled, neither let them be
afraid."

JOHN 14:27

PERSEVERANCE

As for you, brothers, do not grow weary in doing good.

2 THESSALONIANS 3:13

I have fought the good fight, I have finished the race, I have kept the faith.

2 TIMOTHY 4:7

Therefore, my beloved brothers, be steadfast, immovable, always abounding in the work of the Lord, knowing that in the Lord your labor is not in vain.

1 CORINTHIANS 15:58

And you will be hated by all for my name's sake. But the one who endures to the end will be saved.

MARK 13:13

I press on toward the goal for the prize of the upward call of God in Christ Jesus.

PHILIPPIANS 3:14

And let us not grow weary of doing good, for in due season we will reap, if we do not give up.

GALATIANS 6:9

The one who looks into the perfect law, the law of liberty, and perseveres, being no hearer who forgets but a doer who acts, he will be blessed in his doing.

JAMES 1:25

. . . if indeed you continue in the faith, stable and steadfast, not shifting from the hope of the gospel that you heard, which has been proclaimed in all creation under heaven, and of which I, Paul, became a minister.

COLOSSIANS 1:23

Let us hold fast the confession of our hope without wavering, for he who promised is faithful.

HEBREWS 10:23

Therefore, since we are surrounded by so great a cloud of witnesses, let us also lay aside every weight, and sin which clings so closely, and let us run with endurance the race that is set before us, looking to Jesus, the founder and perfecter of our faith, who for the joy that was set before him endured the cross, despising the shame, and is seated at the right hand of the throne of God.

HEBREWS 12:1-2

PRAISE

Sing praises to the LORD, O you his saints,
and give thanks to his holy name.

PSALM 30:4

I call upon the LORD, who is worthy to be praised,
and I am saved from my enemies.

2 SAMUEL 22:4

I will give to the LORD the thanks due to his
righteousness,
and I will sing praise to the name of the LORD,
the Most High.

PSALM 7:17

Through [Jesus] then let us continually offer up a
sacrifice of praise to God, that is, the fruit of lips that
acknowledge his name.

HEBREWS 13:15

My mouth is filled with your praise,
and with your glory all the day.

PSALM 71:8

Blessed are those who dwell in your house,
ever singing your praise!

PSALM 84:4

Then one of them, when he saw that he was healed, turned back, praising God with a loud voice; and he fell on his face at Jesus' feet, giving him thanks. Now he was a Samaritan.

LUKE 17:15-16

Praise the LORD! Praise God in his sanctuary;
    praise him in his mighty heavens!
Praise him for his mighty deeds;
    praise him according to his excellent greatness!

PSALM 150:1-2

What am I to do? I will pray with my spirit, but I will pray with my mind also; I will sing praise with my spirit, but I will sing with my mind also.

1 CORINTHIANS 14:15

Is anyone among you suffering? Let him pray. Is anyone cheerful? Let him sing praise.

JAMES 5:13

I will sing to the LORD as long as I live;
    I will sing praise to my God while I have being.

PSALM 104:33

PRAYER

The LORD is near to all who call on him,
  to all who call on him in truth.

PSALM 145:18

[Jesus said,] "Whatever you ask in prayer, you will receive, if you have faith."

MATTHEW 21:22

"Pray then like this:
Our Father in heaven,
  hallowed be your name.
  Your kingdom come,
  your will be done,
    on earth as it is in heaven.
  Give us this day our daily bread,
  and forgive us our debts,
    as we also have forgiven our debtors.
  And lead us not into temptation,
    but deliver us from evil."

MATTHEW 6:9-13

"Ask, and it will be given to you; seek, and you will find; knock, and it will be opened to you."

MATTHEW 7:7

Likewise the Spirit helps us in our weakness. For we do not know what to pray for as we ought, but the Spirit himself intercedes for us with groaning too deep for words.

ROMANS 8:26

What am I to do? I will pray with my spirit, but I will pray with my mind also; I will sing praise with my spirit, but I will sing with my mind also.

1 CORINTHIANS 14:15

Therefore, confess your sins to one another and pray for one another, that you may be healed. The prayer of a righteous person has great power as it is working.

JAMES 5:16

Let us then with confidence draw near to the throne of grace, that we may receive mercy and find grace to help in time of need.

HEBREWS 4:16

Do not be anxious about anything, but in everything by prayer and supplication with thanksgiving let your requests be made known to God.

PHILIPPIANS 4:6

Pray without ceasing, give thanks in all circumstances; for this is the will of God in Christ Jesus for you.

1 THESSALONIANS 5:17-18

PREDESTINATION

And we know that for those who love God all things work together for good, for those who are called according to his purpose.

ROMANS 8:28

[God] saved us and called us to a holy calling, not because of our works but because of his own purpose and grace, which he gave us in Christ Jesus before the ages began.

2 TIMOTHY 1:9

"You did not choose me, but I chose you and appointed you that you should go and bear fruit and that your fruit should abide, so that whatever you ask the Father in my name, he may give it to you."

JOHN 15:16

[God] chose us in him before the foundation of the world, that we should be holy and blameless before him. In love he predestined us for adoption through Jesus Christ, according to the purpose of his will.

EPHESIANS 1:4-5

For those whom [God] foreknew he also predestined to be conformed to the image of his Son, in order that he might be the firstborn among many brothers.

And those whom he predestined he also called, and those whom he called he also justified, and those whom he justified he also glorified.

ROMANS 8:29-30

For we are his workmanship, created in Christ Jesus for good works, which God prepared beforehand, that we should walk in them.

EPHESIANS 2:10

For you are a people holy to the LORD your God. The LORD your God has chosen you to be a people for his treasured possession, out of all the peoples who are on the face of the earth.

DEUTERONOMY 7:6

In [Christ] we have obtained an inheritance, having been predestined according to the purpose of him who works all things according to the counsel of his will.

EPHESIANS 1:11

Therefore, brothers, be all the more diligent to make your calling and election sure, for if you practice these qualities you will never fall.

2 PETER 1:10

PROSPERITY

In the day of prosperity be joyful, and in the day of adversity consider: God has made the one as well as the other, so that man may not find out anything that will be after him.

ECCLESIASTES 7:14

The plans of the diligent lead surely to abundance,
    but everyone who is hasty comes only to pov-
        erty.
The getting of treasures by a lying tongue
    is a fleeting vapor and a snare of death.

PROVERBS 21:5-6

The reward for humility and fear of the LORD
    is riches and honor and life.

PROVERBS 22:4

The LORD makes poor and makes rich;
    he brings low and he exalts.

1 SAMUEL 2:7

Better is a little with the fear of the LORD
    than great treasure and trouble with it.
Better is a dinner of herbs where love is
    than a fattened ox and hatred with it.

PROVERBS 15:16-17

Do not toil to acquire wealth;
    be discerning enough to desist.
When your eyes light on it, it is gone,
    for suddenly it sprouts wings,
    flying like an eagle toward heaven.

PROVERBS 23:4-5

A faithful man will abound with blessings,
    but whoever hastens to be rich will not go
        unpunished.

PROVERBS 28:20

"Do not lay up for yourselves treasures on earth, where moth and rust destroy and where thieves break in and steal, but lay up for yourselves treasures in heaven, where neither moth nor rust destroys and where thieves do not break in and steal. For where your treasure is, there your heart will be also."

MATTHEW 6:19-21

[The righteous one] is like a tree
    planted by streams of water
that yields its fruit in its season,
    and its leaf does not wither.
In all that he does, he prospers.

PSALM 1:3

PROTECTION

God is our refuge and strength,
a very present help in trouble.

PSALM 46:1

The LORD is a stronghold for the oppressed,
a stronghold in times of trouble.

PSALM 9:9

For God alone my soul waits in silence;
from him comes my salvation.
He only is my rock and my salvation,
my fortress; I shall not be greatly shaken.

PSALM 62:1-2

But the Lord is faithful. He will establish you and guard you against the evil one.

2 THESSALONIANS 3:3

In peace I will both lie down and sleep;
for you alone, O LORD, make me dwell in safety.

PSALM 4:8

But let all who take refuge in you rejoice;
let them ever sing for joy,
and spread your protection over them,
that those who love your name may exult in you.

PSALM 5:11

PROVIDENCE

You cause the grass to grow for the livestock
    and plants for man to cultivate,
that he may bring forth food from the earth

PSALM 104:14

Whatever the LORD pleases, he does,
    in heaven and on earth,
    in the seas and all deeps.
He it is who makes the clouds rise at the end of the
        earth,
    who makes lightnings for the rain
    and brings forth the wind from his storehouses.

PSALM 135:5-7

Many are the plans in the mind of a man,
    but it is the purpose of the LORD that will stand.

PROVERBS 19:21

In him we live and move and have our being

ACTS 17:28

It is God who works in you, both to will and to work
for his good pleasure.

PHILIPPIANS 2:13

PROVISION OF GOD

Yours is the kingdom, O LORD. . . . Both riches and honor come from you, and you rule over all. In your hand are power and might, and in your hand it is to make great and to give strength to all.

1 CHRONICLES 29:11-12

The LORD is my shepherd; I shall not want.

PSALM 23:1

"Do not be anxious, saying, 'What shall we eat?' or 'What shall we drink?' or 'What shall we wear?' For the Gentiles seek after all these things, and your heavenly Father knows that you need them all. But seek first the kingdom of God and his righteousness, and all these things will be added to you."

MATTHEW 6:31-33

God will supply every need of yours according to his riches in glory in Christ Jesus.

PHILIPPIANS 4:19

Every good gift and every perfect gift is from above, coming down from the Father of lights with whom there is no variation or shadow due to change.

JAMES 1:17

PURITY

"Blessed are the pure in heart, for they shall see God."

MATTHEW 5:8

Who can say, "I have made my heart pure;
  I am clean from my sin"?

PROVERBS 20:9

Having purified your souls by your obedience to the truth for a sincere brotherly love, love one another earnestly from a pure heart.

1 PETER 1:22

Put to death therefore what is earthly in you: sexual immorality, impurity, passion, evil desire, and covetousness, which is idolatry.

COLOSSIANS 3:5

Let no one despise you for your youth, but set the believers an example in speech, in conduct, in love, in faith, in purity.

1 TIMOTHY 4:12

So flee youthful passions and pursue righteousness, faith, love, and peace, along with those who call on the Lord from a pure heart.

2 TIMOTHY 2:22

"Come now, let us reason together," says the LORD:
though your sins are like scarlet,
    they shall be as white as snow;
though they are red like crimson,
    they shall become like wool."

ISAIAH 1:18

To the pure, all things are pure, but to the defiled and unbelieving, nothing is pure; but both their minds and their consciences are defiled.

TITUS 1:15

Flee from sexual immorality. Every other sin a person commits is outside the body, but the sexually immoral person sins against his own body.

1 CORINTHIANS 6:18

Purge me with hyssop, and I shall be clean;
    wash me, and I shall be whiter than snow.

PSALM 51:7

Let marriage be held in honor among all, and let the marriage bed be undefiled, for God will judge the sexually immoral and adulterous.

HEBREWS 13:4

Finally, brothers, whatever is true, whatever is honorable, whatever is just, whatever is pure, whatever is lovely, whatever is commendable, if there is any excellence, if there is anything worthy of praise, think about these things.

PHILIPPIANS 4:8

Reconciliation

In Christ God was reconciling the world to himself, not counting their trespasses against them, and entrusting to us the message of reconciliation.

2 CORINTHIANS 5:18-19

Therefore, since we have been justified by faith, we have peace with God through our Lord Jesus Christ.

ROMANS 5:1

"Be reconciled to your brother. . . . Come to terms quickly with your accuser while you are going with him to court, lest your accuser hand you over to the judge, and the judge to the guard, and you be put in prison."

MATTHEW 5:23-25

Finally, brothers, rejoice. Aim for restoration, comfort one another, agree with one another, live in peace; and the God of love and peace will be with you.

2 CORINTHIANS 13:11

When one of you has a grievance against another, does he dare go to law before the unrighteous instead of the saints? Or do you not know that the saints will judge the world? And if the world is to be judged by you, are you incompetent to try trivial cases?

1 CORINTHIANS 6:1-2

REDEMPTION

In [Christ] we have redemption through his blood, the forgiveness of our trespasses, according to the riches of his grace.

EPHESIANS 1:7

"The Son of Man came not to be served but to serve, and to give his life as a ransom for many."

MATTHEW 20:28

[You] are justified by his grace as a gift, through the redemption that is in Christ Jesus.

ROMANS 3:24

When the fullness of time had come, God sent forth his Son, born of woman, born under the law, to redeem those who were under the law, so that we might receive adoption as sons.

GALATIANS 4:4-5

He was wounded for our transgressions;
    he was crushed for our iniquities;
upon him was the chastisement that brought us
        peace,
    and with his stripes we are healed.

ISAIAH 53:5

REFUGE

The LORD is my rock and my fortress and my deliv-
     erer,
   my God, my rock, in whom I take refuge,
my shield, and the horn of my salvation,
   my stronghold and my refuge,
   my savior; you save me from violence.

                              2 SAMUEL 22:2-3

The LORD is the strength of his people;
   he is the saving refuge of his anointed.

                              PSALM 28:8

Oh, taste and see that the LORD is good!
   Blessed is the man who takes refuge in him!

                              PSALM 34:8

God is our refuge and strength,
   a very present help in trouble.

                              PSALM 46:1

He who dwells in the shelter of the Most High
   will abide in the shadow of the Almighty.
I will say to the LORD, "My refuge and my fortress,
   my God, in whom I trust."

                              PSALM 91:1-2

Be merciful to me, O God, be merciful to me,
　　for in you my soul takes refuge;
in the shadow of your wings I will take refuge,
　　till the storms of destruction pass by.

PSALM 57:1

But for me it is good to be near God;
　　I have made the Lord GOD my refuge,
　　that I may tell of all your works.

PSALM 73:28

From the end of the earth I call to you
　　when my heart is faint.
Lead me to the rock
　　that is higher than I,
for you have been my refuge,
　　a strong tower against the enemy.

PSALM 61:2-3

RENEWAL

Create in me a clean heart, O God,
  and renew a right spirit within me.

PSALM 51:10

They who wait for the LORD shall renew their strength;
  they shall mount up with wings like eagles;
they shall run and not be weary;
  they shall walk and not faint.

ISAIAH 40:31

And we all, with unveiled face, beholding the glory of
the Lord, are being transformed into the same image
from one degree of glory to another. For this comes
from the Lord who is the Spirit.

2 CORINTHIANS 3:18

Do not be conformed to this world, but be transformed by the renewal of your mind, that by testing
you may discern what is the will of God, what is good
and acceptable and perfect.

ROMANS 12:2

[God] saved us, not because of works done by us in
righteousness, but according to his own mercy, by the
washing of regeneration and renewal of the Holy Spirit.

TITUS 3:5

REPENTANCE

"The time is fulfilled, and the kingdom of God is at hand; repent and believe in the gospel."

MARK 1:15

"Those whom I love, I reprove and discipline, so be zealous and repent."

REVELATION 3:19

If my people who are called by my name humble themselves, and pray and seek my face and turn from their wicked ways, then I will hear from heaven and will forgive their sin and heal their land.

2 CHRONICLES 7:14

"I have not come to call the righteous but sinners to repentance."

LUKE 5:32

The Lord is not slow to fulfill his promise as some count slowness, but is patient toward you, not wishing that any should perish, but that all should reach repentance.

2 PETER 3:9

"There will be more joy in heaven over one sinner who repents than over ninety-nine righteous persons who need no repentance."

LUKE 15:7

REST

"Come to me, all who labor and are heavy laden, and I will give you rest. Take my yoke upon you, and learn from me, for I am gentle and lowly in heart, and you will find rest for your souls. For my yoke is easy, and my burden is light."

MATTHEW 11:28-30

Six days you shall do your work, but on the seventh day you shall rest.

EXODUS 23:12

Return, O my soul, to your rest;
    for the LORD has dealt bountifully with you.

PSALM 116:7

While the promise of entering [Christ's] rest still stands, let us fear lest any of [us] should seem to have failed to reach it.

HEBREWS 4:1

So then, there remains a Sabbath rest for the people of God.

HEBREWS 4:9

RESURRECTION

"As the Father raises the dead and gives them life, so also the Son gives life to whom he will."

JOHN 5:21

Your dead shall live; their bodies shall rise.
> You who dwell in the dust, awake and sing for
> > joy!
For your dew is a dew of light,
> and the earth will give birth to the dead.

ISAIAH 26:19

And Jesus said to them, "The sons of this age marry and are given in marriage, but those who are considered worthy to attain to that age and to the resurrection from the dead neither marry nor are given in marriage, for they cannot die anymore, because they are equal to angels and are sons of God, being sons of the resurrection."

LUKE 20:34-36

"An hour is coming when all who are in the tombs will hear [the Son of Man's] voice and come out, those who have done good to the resurrection of life, and those who have done evil to the resurrection of judgment."

JOHN 5:28-29

For I delivered to you as of first importance what I also received: that Christ died for our sins in accordance with the Scriptures, that he was buried, that he was raised on the third day in accordance with the Scriptures.

1 CORINTHIANS 15:3-4

And after my skin has been thus destroyed,
   yet in my flesh I shall see God,
whom I shall see for myself,
   and my eyes shall behold, and not another.
My heart faints within me!

JOB 19:26-27

And [Jesus] was declared to be the Son of God in power according to the Spirit of holiness by his resurrection from the dead, Jesus Christ our Lord.

ROMANS 1:4

God raised [Christ] up, loosing the pangs of death, because it was not possible for him to be held by it.

ACTS 2:24

[David] foresaw and spoke about the resurrection of the Christ, that he was not abandoned to Hades, nor did his flesh see corruption.

ACTS 2:31

We were buried therefore with [Christ] by baptism into death, in order that, just as Christ was raised from the dead by the glory of the Father, we too might walk in newness of life.

ROMANS 6:4

If then you have been raised with Christ, seek the things that are above, where Christ is, seated at the right hand of God.

COLOSSIANS 3:1

If the Spirit of him who raised Jesus from the dead dwells in you, he who raised Christ Jesus from the dead will also give life to your mortal bodies through his Spirit who dwells in you.

ROMANS 8:11

Jesus said to her, "I am the resurrection and the life. Whoever believes in me, though he die, yet shall he live."

JOHN 11:25

For since we believe that Jesus died and rose again, even so, through Jesus, God will bring with him those who have fallen asleep.

1 THESSALONIANS 4:14

REVIVAL

And in the last days it shall be, God declares,
that I will pour out my Spirit on all flesh,
    and your sons and your daughters shall
        prophesy,
and your young men shall see visions,
    and your old men shall dream dreams.

ACTS 2:17

You who have made me see many troubles and
        calamities
    will revive me again;
from the depths of the earth
    you will bring me up again.

PSALM 71:20

Turn my eyes from looking at worthless things;
    and give me life in your ways.

PSALM 119:37

In your steadfast love give me life,
    that I may keep the testimonies of your mouth.

PSALM 119:88

Create in me a clean heart, O God,
    and renew a right spirit within me.

PSALM 51:10

Jesus answered him, "Truly, truly, I say to you, unless one is born again he cannot see the kingdom of God."

JOHN 3:3

Therefore, if anyone is in Christ, he is a new creation. The old has passed away; behold, the new has come.

2 CORINTHIANS 5:17

[Christ] saved us, not because of works done by us in righteousness, but according to his own mercy, by the washing of regeneration and renewal of the Holy Spirit.

TITUS 3:5

Will you not revive us again,
    that your people may rejoice in you?

PSALM 85:6

REWARDS

~~~~~

"Rejoice and be glad, for your reward is great in heaven, for so they persecuted the prophets who were before you."

MATTHEW 5:12

"For the Son of Man is going to come with his angels in the glory of his Father, and then he will repay each person according to what he has done."

MATTHEW 16:27

For we must all appear before the judgment seat of Christ, so that each one may receive what is due for what he has done in the body, whether good or evil.

2 CORINTHIANS 5:10

[Moses] . . . considered the reproach of Christ greater wealth than the treasures of Egypt, for he was looking to the reward.

HEBREWS 11:26

Do you not know that in a race all the runners compete, but only one receives the prize? So run that you may obtain it.

1 CORINTHIANS 9:24

And without faith it is impossible to please him, for whoever would draw near to God must believe that he exists and that he rewards those who seek him.

HEBREWS 11:6

I have fought the good fight, I have finished the race, I have kept the faith. Henceforth there is laid up for me the crown of righteousness, which the Lord, the righteous judge, will award to me on that Day, and not only to me but also to all who have loved his appearing.

2 TIMOTHY 4:7-8

For the wages of sin is death, but the free gift of God is eternal life in Christ Jesus our Lord.

ROMANS 6:23

Righteousness

"Blessed are those who hunger and thirst for righteousness, for they shall be satisfied."

MATTHEW 5:6

And [Abram] believed the Lord, and he counted it to him as righteousness.

GENESIS 15:6

But as for you, O man of God, flee these things. Pursue righteousness, godliness, faith, love, steadfastness, gentleness.

1 TIMOTHY 6:11

None is righteous, no, not one.

ROMANS 3:10

For the Lord is righteous;
he loves righteous deeds;
    the upright shall behold his face.

PSALM 11:7

So flee youthful passions and pursue righteousness, faith, love, and peace, along with those who call on the Lord from a pure heart.

2 TIMOTHY 2:22

The prayer of a righteous person has great power as it is working.

JAMES 5:16

For the eyes of the Lord are on the righteous,
  and his ears are open to their prayer.

1 PETER 3:12

For I am not ashamed of the gospel, for it is the power of God for salvation to everyone who believes, to the Jew first and also to the Greek. For in it the righteousness of God is revealed from faith for faith, as it is written, "The righteous shall live by faith."

ROMANS 1:16-17

Therefore, as one trespass led to condemnation for all men, so one act of righteousness leads to justification and life for all men.

ROMANS 5:18

[God] saved us, not because of works done by us in righteousness, but according to his own mercy, by the washing of regeneration and renewal of the Holy Spirit.

TITUS 3:5

Henceforth there is laid up for me the crown of righteousness, which the Lord, the righteous judge, will award to me on that Day, and not only to me but also to all who have loved his appearing.

2 TIMOTHY 4:8

SALVATION

If you confess with your mouth that Jesus is Lord and believe in your heart that God raised him from the dead, you will be saved.

ROMANS 10:9

"[Mary] will bear a son, and you shall call his name Jesus, for he will save his people from their sins."

MATTHEW 1:21

And [Jesus] said to the woman, "Your faith has saved you; go in peace."

LUKE 7:50

"For God so loved the world, that he gave his only Son, that whoever believes in him should not perish but have eternal life. For God did not send his Son into the world to condemn the world, but in order that the world might be saved through him.

JOHN 3:16-17

And it shall come to pass that everyone who calls upon the name of the Lord shall be saved.

ACTS 2:21

Since, therefore, we have now been justified by his blood, much more shall we be saved by him from the wrath of God. For if while we were enemies we were reconciled to God by the death of his Son, much more, now that we are reconciled, shall we be saved by his life.

ROMANS 5:9-10

I am not ashamed of the gospel, for it is the power of God for salvation to everyone who believes

ROMANS 1:16

Then he brought them out and said, "Sirs, what must I do to be saved?" And they said, "Believe in the Lord Jesus, and you will be saved, you and your household."

ACTS 16:30-31

Work out your own salvation with fear and trembling, for it is God who works in you, both to will and to work for his good pleasure.

PHILIPPIANS 2:12b-13

By grace you have been saved through faith. And this is not your own doing; it is the gift of God.

EPHESIANS 2:8

SANCTIFICATION

Now that you have been set free from sin and have become slaves of God, the fruit you get leads to sanctification and its end, eternal life.

ROMANS 6:22

Christ loved the church and gave himself up for her, that he might sanctify her, having cleansed her by the washing of water with the word.

EPHESIANS 5:25-26

Therefore, if anyone cleanses himself from what is dishonorable, he will be a vessel for honorable use, set apart as holy, useful to the master of the house, ready for every good work.

2 TIMOTHY 2:21

May the God of peace himself sanctify you completely, and may your whole spirit and soul and body be kept blameless at the coming of our Lord Jesus Christ. He who calls you is faithful; he will surely do it.

1 THESSALONIANS 5:23-24

SECURITY

"My Father, who has given them to me, is greater than all, and no one is able to snatch them out of the Father's hand."

JOHN 10:29

He drew me up from the pit of destruction,
    out of the miry bog,
and set my feet upon a rock,
    making my steps secure.

PSALM 40:2

"Surely then you will lift up your face without
        blemish;
    you will be secure and will not fear."

JOB 11:15

What then shall we say to these things? If God is for us, who can be against us?

ROMANS 8:31

For I am sure that neither death nor life, nor angels nor rulers, nor things present nor things to come, nor powers, nor height nor depth, nor anything else in all creation, will be able to separate us from the love of God in Christ Jesus our Lord.

ROMANS 8:38-39

He made my feet like the feet of a deer
  and set me secure on the heights.

2 SAMUEL 22:34

He who dwells in the shelter of the Most High
  will abide in the shadow of the Almighty.
I will say to the LORD, "My refuge and my fortress,
  my God, in whom I trust."

PSALM 91:1-2

Therefore my heart is glad, and my whole being
        rejoices;
  my flesh also dwells secure.

PSALM 16:9

SELFLESSNESS

Do nothing from rivalry or conceit, but in humility count others more significant than yourselves. Let each of you look not only to his own interests, but also to the interests of others.

PHILIPPIANS 2:3-4

We who are strong have an obligation to bear with the failings of the weak, and not to please ourselves. Let each of us please his neighbor for his good, to build him up.

ROMANS 15:1-2

Let no one seek his own good, but the good of his neighbor.

1 CORINTHIANS 10:24

Love is patient and kind; love does not envy or boast; it is not arrogant or rude. It does not insist on its own way; it is not irritable or resentful.

1 CORINTHIANS 13:4-5

"The second [commandment] is this: 'You shall love your neighbor as yourself.' There is no other commandment greater than these."

MARK 12:31

SERVICE

For you were called to freedom, brothers. Only do not use your freedom as an opportunity for the flesh, but through love serve one another.

GALATIANS 5:13

Do nothing from rivalry or conceit, but in humility count others more significant than yourselves. Let each of you look not only to his own interests, but also to the interests of others.

PHILIPPIANS 2:3-4

"Even the Son of Man came not to be served but to serve, and to give his life as a ransom for many."

MARK 10:45

"Then the righteous will answer him, saying, 'Lord, when did we see you hungry and feed you, or thirsty and give you drink? And when did we see you a stranger and welcome you, or naked and clothe you? And when did we see you sick or in prison and visit you?' And the King will answer them, 'Truly, I say to you, as you did it to one of the least of these my brothers, you did it to me.'"

MATTHEW 25:37-40

SHARING FAITH

"Go therefore and make disciples of all nations, baptizing them in the name of the Father and of the Son and of the Holy Spirit."

MATTHEW 28:19

In your hearts regard Christ the Lord as holy, always being prepared to make a defense to anyone who asks you for a reason for the hope that is in you.

1 PETER 3:15

Preach the word; be ready in season and out of season; reprove, rebuke, and exhort, with complete patience and teaching.

2 TIMOTHY 4:2

How beautiful are the feet of those who preach the good news!

ROMANS 10:15

STEWARDSHIP

It is required of stewards that they be found trust-worthy.

1 CORINTHIANS 4:2

The point is this: whoever sows sparingly will also reap sparingly, and whoever sows bountifully will also reap bountifully. Each one must give as he has made up his mind, not reluctantly or under compulsion, for God loves a cheerful giver.

2 CORINTHIANS 9:6-7

As each has received a gift, use it to serve one another, as good stewards of God's varied grace.

1 PETER 4:10

He who supplies seed to the sower and bread for food will supply and multiply your seed for sowing and increase the harvest of your righteousness.

2 CORINTHIANS 9:10

By the Holy Spirit who dwells within us, guard the good deposit entrusted to you.

2 TIMOTHY 1:14

Strength

❧

Even youths shall faint and be weary,
    and young men shall fall exhausted;
but they who wait for the Lord shall renew their
        strength;
    they shall mount up with wings like eagles;
they shall run and not be weary;
    they shall walk and not faint.

ISAIAH 40:30-31

But he said to me, "My grace is sufficient for you, for
my power is made perfect in weakness." Therefore I
will boast all the more gladly of my weaknesses, so
that the power of Christ may rest upon me.

2 CORINTHIANS 12:9

For God gave us a spirit not of fear but of power and
love and self-control.

2 TIMOTHY 1:7

Be strong in the Lord and in the strength of his might.

PSALM 29:11

May the Lord give strength to his people!
    May the Lord bless his people with peace!

EPHESIANS 6:10

SUBMISSION

Submit yourselves therefore to God. Resist the devil, and he will flee from you.

JAMES 4:7

Be filled with the Spirit . . . submitting to one another out of reverence for Christ.

EPHESIANS 5:18,21

Children, obey your parents in the Lord, for this is right.

EPHESIANS 6:1

Now as the church submits to Christ, so also wives should submit in everything to their husbands.

EPHESIANS 5:24

Obey your leaders and submit to them, for they are keeping watch over your souls, as those who will have to give an account. Let them do this with joy and not with groaning, for that would be of no advantage to you.

HEBREWS 13:17

Let every person be subject to the governing authorities. For there is no authority except from God, and those that exist have been instituted by God.

ROMANS 13:1

THANKSGIVING

Give thanks in all circumstances; for this is the will of God in Christ Jesus for you.

1 THESSALONIANS 5:18

Sing praises to the LORD, O you his saints,
    and give thanks to his holy name.

PSALM 30:4

Do not be anxious about anything, but in everything by prayer and supplication with thanksgiving let your requests be made known to God.

PHILIPPIANS 4:6

Offer to God a sacrifice of thanksgiving,
    and perform your vows to the Most High.

PSALM 50:14

Thanks be to God, who gives us the victory through our Lord Jesus Christ.

1 CORINTHIANS 15:57

And whatever you do, in word or deed, do everything in the name of the Lord Jesus, giving thanks to God the Father through him.

COLOSSIANS 3:17

Give thanks to the LORD, for he is good,
for his steadfast love endures forever.

PSALM 136:1

Thanks be to God for his inexpressible gift!

2 CORINTHIANS 9:15

Continue steadfastly in prayer, being watchful in it
with thanksgiving.

COLOSSIANS 4:2

Let us come into his presence with thanksgiving;
let us make a joyful noise to him with songs of
praise!

PSALM 95:2

TRUST

I have trusted in your steadfast love;
  my heart shall rejoice in your salvation.

PSALM 13:5

Trust in him at all times, O people;
  pour out your heart before him;
  God is a refuge for us.

PSALM 62:8

Commit your way to the LORD;
  trust in him, and he will act.

PSALM 37:5

In God I trust; I shall not be afraid.
  What can man do to me?

PSALM 56:11

Behold, God is my salvation;
  I will trust, and will not be afraid;
for the LORD GOD is my strength and my song,
  and he has become my salvation.

ISAIAH 12:2

It is better to take refuge in the LORD
  than to trust in princes.

PSALM 118:9

Those who trust in the Lord are like Mount Zion,
    which cannot be moved, but abides forever.

PSALM 125:1

Trust in the Lord with all your heart,
    and do not lean on your own understanding.

PROVERBS 3:5

Blessed is the man who trusts in the Lord,
    whose trust is the Lord.
He is like a tree planted by water,
    that sends out its roots by the stream,
and does not fear when heat comes,
    for its leaves remain green,
and is not anxious in the year of drought,
    for it does not cease to bear fruit.

JEREMIAH 17:7-8

TRUTH

Jesus said to him, "I am the way, and the truth, and the life. No one comes to the Father except through me."

JOHN 14:6

Whoever speaks the truth gives honest evidence,
  but a false witness utters deceit.

PROVERBS 12:17

Speak the truth to one another; render in your gates judgments that are true and make for peace.

ZECHARIAH 8:16

Finally, brothers, whatever is true, whatever is honorable, whatever is just, whatever is pure, whatever is lovely, whatever is commendable, if there is any excellence, if there is anything worthy of praise, think about these things.

PHILIPPIANS 4:8

Stand therefore, having fastened on the belt of truth, and having put on the breastplate of righteousness.

EPHESIANS 6:14

The rules of the LORD are true,
  and righteous altogether.

PSALM 19:9

So Jesus said to the Jews who had believed in him, "If you abide in my word, you are truly my disciples, and you will know the truth, and the truth will set you free."

JOHN 8:31-32

Do your best to present yourself to God as one approved, a worker who has no need to be ashamed, rightly handling the word of truth.

2 TIMOTHY 2:15

"God is spirit, and those who worship him must worship in spirit and truth."

JOHN 4:24

"When the Spirit of truth comes, he will guide you into all the truth, for he will not speak on his own authority, but whatever he hears he will speak, and he will declare to you the things that are to come."

JOHN 16:13

UNDERSTANDING

The LORD by wisdom founded the earth;
    by understanding he established the heavens.

PROVERBS 3:19

"Wisdom is with the aged,
    and understanding in length of days.
With God are wisdom and might;
    he has counsel and understanding."

JOB 12:12-13

"Behold, the fear of the Lord, that is wisdom,
    and to turn away from evil is understanding."

JOB 28:28

"It is the spirit in man,
    the breath of the Almighty, that makes him
        understand."

JOB 32:8

Let my cry come before you, O LORD;
    give me understanding according to your word!

PSALM 119:169

On the lips of him who has understanding, wisdom
        is found.

PROVERBS 10:13

I have more understanding than all my teachers,
for your testimonies are my meditation.
I understand more than the aged,
for I keep your precepts.

PSALM 119:99-100

The unfolding of your words gives light;
it imparts understanding to the simple.

PSALM 119:130

At that time Jesus declared, "I thank you, Father,
Lord of heaven and earth, that you have hidden
these things from the wise and understanding and
revealed them to little children."

MATTHEW 11:25

The purpose in a man's heart is like deep water,
but a man of understanding will draw it out.

PROVERBS 20:5

Have you not known? Have you not heard?
The LORD is the everlasting God,
the Creator of the ends of the earth.
He does not faint or grow weary;
his understanding is unsearchable.

ISAIAH 40:28

Trust in the LORD with all your heart,
and do not lean on your own understanding.

PROVERBS 3:5

UNITY

Behold, how good and pleasant it is
  when brothers dwell in unity!

PSALM 133:1

Now the full number of those who believed were of one heart and soul, and no one said that any of the things that belonged to him was his own, but they had everything in common.

ACTS 4:32

Live in harmony with one another. Do not be haughty, but associate with the lowly. Never be conceited.

ROMANS 12:16

So then let us pursue what makes for peace and for mutual upbuilding.

ROMANS 14:19

May the God of endurance and encouragement grant you to live in such harmony with one another, in accord with Christ Jesus, that together you may with one voice glorify the God and Father of our Lord Jesus Christ.

ROMANS 15:5-6

I appeal to you, brothers, by the name of our Lord Jesus Christ, that all of you agree and that there be no divisions among you, but that you be united in the same mind and the same judgment.

1 CORINTHIANS 1:10

There is one body and one Spirit—just as you were called to the one hope that belongs to your call—one Lord, one faith, one baptism, one God and Father of all, who is over all and through all and in all.

EPHESIANS 4:4-6

Let your manner of life be worthy of the gospel of Christ, so that whether I come and see you or am absent, I may hear of you that you are standing firm in one spirit, with one mind striving side by side for the faith of the gospel.

PHILIPPIANS 1:27

"I do not ask for these only, but also for those who will believe in me through their word, that they may all be one, just as you, Father, are in me, and I in you, that they also may be in us, so that the world may believe that you have sent me."

JOHN 17:20-21

Finally, all of you, have unity of mind, sympathy, brotherly love, a tender heart, and a humble mind.

1 PETER 3:8

VICTORY OVER SIN

[Jesus said,] "In the world you will have tribulation. But take heart; I have overcome the world."

JOHN 16:33

In all these things we are more than conquerors through him who loved us.

ROMANS 8:37

You are from God and have overcome [evil], for he who is in you is greater than he who is in the world.

1 JOHN 4:4

[Jesus prayed,] "And lead us not into temptation, but deliver us from evil."

MATTHEW 6:13

For everyone who has been born of God overcomes the world. And this is the victory that has overcome the world—our faith.

1 JOHN 5:4

WILL OF GOD

[Jesus prayed,] "Your kingdom come,
your will be done,
on earth as it is in heaven."

MATTHEW 6:10

"For whoever does the will of my Father in heaven is
my brother and sister and mother."

MATTHEW 12:50

And [Jesus] said, "Abba, Father, all things are possible for you. Remove this cup from me. Yet not what
I will, but what you will."

MARK 14:36

Jesus said to them, "My food is to do the will of him
who sent me and to accomplish his work."

JOHN 4:34

And the world is passing away along with its desires,
but whoever does the will of God abides forever.

1 JOHN 2:17

And this is the confidence that we have toward him,
that if we ask anything according to his will he hears
us.

1 JOHN 5:14

Do not be conformed to this world, but be transformed by the renewal of your mind, that by testing you may discern what is the will of God, what is good and acceptable and perfect.

ROMANS 12:2

[Jesus said,] "For I have come down from heaven, not to do my own will but the will of him who sent me. And this is the will of him who sent me, that I should lose nothing of all that he has given me, but raise it up on the last day. For this is the will of my Father, that everyone who looks on the Son and believes in him should have eternal life, and I will raise him up on the last day."

JOHN 6:38-40

WISDOM FOR LIFE

"But it is the spirit in man,
   the breath of the Almighty, that makes him
      understand.
It is not the old who are wise,
   nor the aged who understand what is right."

JOB 32:8-9

Who is wise and understanding among you? By his good conduct let him show his works in the meekness of wisdom.

JAMES 3:13

The fear of the LORD is the beginning of knowledge; fools despise wisdom and instruction.

PROVERBS 1:7

[Jesus said,] "Everyone then who hears these words of mine and does them will be like a wise man who built his house on the rock."

MATTHEW 7:24

If any of you lacks wisdom, let him ask God, who gives generously to all without reproach, and it will be given him.

JAMES 1:5

WISDOM OF GOD

Oh, the depth of the riches and wisdom and knowledge of God! How unsearchable are his judgments and how inscrutable his ways!

ROMANS 11:33

The LORD by wisdom founded the earth;
  by understanding he established the heavens.

PROVERBS 3:19

"Behold, God is mighty, and does not despise any;
  he is mighty in strength of understanding."

JOB 36:5

We impart a secret and hidden wisdom of God, which God decreed before the ages for our glory.

1 CORINTHIANS 2:7

"Blessed be the name of God forever and ever,
  to whom belong wisdom and might."

DANIEL 2:20

God . . . created all things, so that through the church the manifold wisdom of God might now be made known to the rulers and authorities in the heavenly places.

EPHESIANS 3:8-10

Work

"By the sweat of your face
   you shall eat bread,
till you return to the ground,
   for out of it you were taken;
for you are dust,
   and to dust you shall return."

GENESIS 3:19

Six days you shall labor, and do all your work, but the seventh day is a Sabbath to the Lord your God. On it you shall not do any work.

EXODUS 20:9-10

Sweet is the sleep of a laborer, whether he eats little or much, but the full stomach of the rich will not let him sleep.

ECCLESIASTES 5:12

Aspire to live quietly, and to mind your own affairs, and to work with your hands, as we instructed you, so that you may live properly before outsiders and be dependent on no one.

1 THESSALONIANS 4:11-12

For you yourselves know how you ought to imitate us, because we were not idle when we were with you,

nor did we eat anyone's bread without paying for it,
but with toil and labor we worked night and day,
that we might not be a burden to any of you.

2 THESSALONIANS 3:7-8

"In all things I have shown you that by working hard
in this way we must help the weak and remember
the words of the Lord Jesus, how he himself said, 'It
is more blessed to give than to receive.'"

ACTS 20:35

Whoever works his land will have plenty of bread,
but he who follows worthless pursuits lacks
sense.

PROVERBS 12:11

Commit your work to the LORD,
and your plans will be established.

PROVERBS 16:3

WORSHIP

You shall worship no other god, for the LORD, whose name is Jealous, is a jealous God.

EXODUS 34:14

"But the hour is coming, and is now here, when the true worshipers will worship the Father in spirit and truth, for the Father is seeking such people to worship him."

JOHN 4:23

Then Jesus said to him, "Be gone, Satan! For it is written,
"'You shall worship the Lord your God
and him only shall you serve.'"

MATTHEW 4:10

Ascribe to the LORD the glory due his name;
bring an offering, and come into his courts!
Worship the LORD in the splendor of holiness;
tremble before him, all the earth!

PSALM 96:8-9

I will pray with my spirit, but I will pray with my mind also; I will sing praise with my spirit, but I will sing with my mind also.

1 CORINTHIANS 14:15

Therefore let us be grateful for receiving a kingdom that cannot be shaken, and thus let us offer to God acceptable worship, with reverence and awe.

HEBREWS 12:28

All the ends of the earth shall remember
    and turn to the LORD,
and all the families of the nations
    shall worship before you.

PSALM 22:27

All the nations you have made shall come
    and worship before you, O Lord,
    and shall glorify your name.

PSALM 86:9

I appeal to you therefore, brothers, by the mercies of God, to present your bodies as a living sacrifice, holy and acceptable to God, which is your spiritual worship. Do not be conformed to this world, but be transformed by the renewal of your mind, that by testing you may discern what is the will of God, what is good and acceptable and perfect.

ROMANS 12:1-2

ALSO AVAILABLE

Compiled from the ESV® Bible, *The Bible's Promises for Women* puts God's promises at your fingertips. The book is arranged by topic and is easy to navigate—making it a perfect gift for any woman who wants to know God and his Word better.